The Portable Coach:

A Do-It-Yourself Approach to Personal Coaching

Lorraine C. Enos

PageFree Publishing, Inc.

ISBN: 1-930252-95-1
Trade Paperback
Published May 2002

E-Book ISBN: 1-58200-018-2
Published 1998

PageFree Publishing, Inc.
733 Howard Street
Otsego, MI 49078

http://www.pagefreepublishing.com

To John, Sean, and Caitlin. Thanks for loving me and being there through the tough times and the good times.

Table of Contents

Acknowledgments

I feel as if I've just won an Oscar and have only been given thirty seconds to thank all of the people who've made this book possible. Starting is easy, it's making sure I don't forget anyone that is the hard part.

My husband, John, has been my staunchest supporter throughout the writing process. He's believed in me and encouraged me when I wasn't sure I could finish The Portable Coach or that it was a worthwhile endeavor. He's also been my toughest critic. He's read through my book a dozen times to make sure I don't have run-on sentences and have used my commas correctly. Thanks for being there for me.

Sean and Caitlin, my beautiful and delightful children, have been understanding (usually) when Mommy can't play with them because I'm glued to my computer. They've encouraged me and given me hope when life has looked bleak.

My parents have always believed in me and supported my writing. At times, they've wished I would pursue a nice safe career and I'm sure there are days that they've wished I would get my act together. I only wish that I could write with half as much passion and feeling as my dad.

To all the bosses I've ever had who weren't sure quite how to handle me. Thanks. I've had bosses who have been incredibly encouraging and others who I wanted to shoot. You know who you are.

Lastly, I owe a huge debt of gratitude to the United States military for proving to me that I could live through hell and come out on the other side a stronger and wiser person.

What possessed me to write this book?

Like many people who are unsatisfied with their lives and want to change, I've always had the nagging feeling that I wasn't living the life I was meant to live. There have been times in my life when I've made great money, other times when I made barely enough to pay the bills, but regardless of my financial situation, I've never felt as if I was fulfilling my life's purpose.

In my search for self I turned to self-help books and new age techniques, and then spent hours berating myself because these techniques didn't provide me with instant gratification. I thought about consulting a personal coach to walk me through life changes, but I couldn't afford their fees, which can range from $75.00 to $200.00 an hour. I had to go it alone and figure out how to get what I wanted. Over the next several years, I spent long nights and teary days crying over the prototypes of these exercises. My biggest breakthrough was when I realized that before I could figure out who I wanted to become, I had to figure out who I was. I did some deep soul searching to find out what my strengths and weaknesses were, what I felt was important, and what I was willing to do to change my life.

Most of the "How to Change Your Life" books I've read make it sound easy: Meditation, positive thinking, or visualization alone were supposed to be enough to make real and lasting changes. One book I read in particular stands out because the author was able to completely transform his life in two years. However, after finishing the book, I became disillusioned because I realized that the only reason this author was able to transform himself was because he didn't work for the entire two years but had someone else pay the bills while he worked on improving himself. Unfortunately, the rest of us aren't that lucky: we still have families to support and bills to pay and can't afford to take a year off from our responsibilities. The Portable Coach was written to help you bridge that gap and make real and lasting changes while you support your family and pay your bills.

To convince you I've been there and know what you are going through let me tell you my story. I grew up in a middle class family. My parents made sacrifices to put me through college. I got an accounting degree because it was practical and I'd always be able to support myself. The only problem was I hated accounting. Through dumb luck I landed a well paying job as an auditor for the U.S. Government. About the same time, I drifted into marriage. We'd only been married a year when I found myself drifting into motherhood. Because my job paid better, we decided I would continue working and John would stay home with the baby. Shortly after Sean was born, I was offered a position in Okinawa and we traveled overseas. Three years and another baby later, I gave up my well paying job and we returned to the States. Upon returning to the States we spent more time drifting. We moved constantly and I never found a job I loved. I kept thinking that my ship was just a little late arriving at the dock but eventually everything would fall into place like it always had. It never occurred to me to swim out and meet the ship.

I finally gave up on waiting for my ship to come in and sat down and charted the difference between where I was and where I wanted to be. I realized it would take some work and sacrifice to become a self-employed writer but it was possible. This was when I developed my seed theory of self-improvement, which is based upon the Tao principle of detachment. Instead of planting one seed and devoting all of my time and energy nurturing that one seed and being disappointed when it fails to blossom, I plant as many seeds as I can and then nurture the ones that grow. For instance, if I'm looking for a job, I send out resumes for jobs I think would be interesting. Instead of getting my heart set on one job and being heartbroken when it falls through, I blanket the market with resumes and wait until I start getting results. Once I get interviews, I give it my all but still keep my options open until I get a job offer. I've been saved a lot of heartache and false hope by practicing detachment.

Another insight that came to me was the realization that I didn't want a "real" job. I hated the thought of being tied to one job for an undetermined amount of time. What I really wanted to do was share these insights and help other people change their lives. I decided to take jobs that required little emotional investment to pay the bills and put my energy into writing The Portable Coach. I owed it to myself to give my dreams the best chance possible. I started working for temp agencies and learned a surprising lesson: a lot of temp jobs just required a presence to answer phones, etc. As long as I did what was asked of me, I had free time to work on writing my book.

You hold in your hands the finished product of my heartache and struggle. I hope that the lessons I've learned will help you make the changes you need or want to make in your life.

How to Use this Book

This book is your Personal Life Coach and with a little bit of time and effort, it can help you change your life. The Portable Coach is written in a workbook format to give you a place to record your hopes, your dreams, your problems, your false starts, and your accomplishments. There are several ways you can use this book.

- ☯ You can record all of your answers in the book and refer back to it when you face your next challenge.
- ☯ You can use a three-ring binder to record your progress and rearrange the pages as required.
- ☯ You can record your answers in the book and rip out the pages you want to keep with you. If you need more copies of a particular work sheet, feel free to make them.

Several times throughout the book, you'll be asked to use a highlighter to track your answers. I'd suggest using several colors of highlighters and assigning each a particular meaning.

I'm not arrogant or pompous enough to claim to have all the answers. The true answers to your life lie in your heart. My job is to help you find your own truth. Making changes in your life is hard, and the answers are different for each person. To get to the right answers you need to ask the right questions. This could be a long process, because each answer generally uncovers another question.

The most important thing to remember is:

YOU CAN DO THIS!!

Self Knowledge

On my journey through life, I've learned that knowing who you are is at least as important as knowing who you want to become. I've always been a dreamer whose specialty was coming up with grandiose schemes to change my life. Nothing worked until I took a long hard look in the mirror and assessed who I was and what talents, passions, fears, hang-ups, etc. I possessed. Some of my personal qualities I've chosen to embrace, others I've worked to change, and some I've had to learn to live with. Deciding who you want to become without assessing what you have is like deciding you want to make a gourmet dinner without assessing your cooking skills, the food in your pantry, and the utensils you have on hand. Without the proper assessment and preparation, instead of a gourmet meal, you'll end up with a big mess that could take longer to clean up than the extra prep time would have taken.

The exercises in this section are designed to give you an idea of who you are and could spawn even more soul searching. Be honest with yourself as you work through this book. Some of the information you uncover may be painful, some may make you proud, but you must take the good and the bad. Remember, there are no right or wrong answers, only honest or dishonest ones. Truthful answers will help you become who you were meant to be. If you are working through these exercises and find yourself starting to write down dishonest answers because you can't face the truth, take a deep breath and remember the only person dishonesty will hurt is you. I know the process can be painful, but trust me, it's worth the trip.

As you begin this journey of self, you'll be looking at the following:

Outer Images: People often assess us based on the persona we present to the world and make judgments based on the clothing we wear, where we live, our marital status, and our material possessions. Any self assessment would be incomplete if it failed to take into account the outer image you present to the world.

Self Description: Your self description will provide you with two valuable pieces of information: What your self image is and if you are physically capable of obtaining your goals.

Likes and Dislikes: In this exercise, you'll look at the things you love and hate about yourself. What traits do you want to keep and which do you want to eliminate?

Passions, Talents, and Skills: The path to true happiness is often found by using your skills and talents to support your passion. In these exercises you will identify what you love, what you have a natural talent for, what skills you have honed, and figure out how to use your talents and skills to support your passion.

Priorities: Human beings are complex creatures and you might have conflicting priorities. Identifying potential conflicts and assessing what is truly important to you can help you set realistic goals that are in line with your priorities.

Fears: Fears can help or hinder you on your journey to self-fulfillment. Some fears can help you avoid harmful situations, but other, often unfounded, fears can hinder your personal growth. By identifying realistic fears and rooting out self-defeating fears, you can minimize the fears that are standing in your way.

Emotions: Your emotional style and how you express or suppress your emotions can play a role in your success or failure in life. These exercises will help you identify your emotional style and assess what's working and what's not.

False Jealousy: We are all jealous of someone. Sometimes this jealousy is justified and sometimes it isn't. I define False Jealousy as being jealous of things that we cannot realistically obtain.

Risk Taking: Are you a risk-taker or do you prefer working with a safety net? These exercises will help identify your comfort with risk.

Operational Style: Some people are born leaders and others prefer to follow. These exercises will help determine your preferred modus operandi.

Self Confidence: Are you confident of your abilities and engage in occasional bouts of "Shameless Self-Promotion" or do you cower in a corner when someone recognizes your accomplishments?

Comfort Zone: All of the above factors help determine your comfort zone. I've included a summary section for quick reference when you're working on your goal setting.

By the time you have finished this section, you should have an honest, realistic view of who you are, what you need to change, and what you like about yourself.

Good luck as you begin this journey of self.

Outer Images

We all have a persona that by choice or circumstance we show the outer world. This persona is reflected in a person's living arrangements, marital status, and possessions. Sometimes, these items are the result of deliberate choices we've made in our lives. Other times we drift into situations by letting the world and/or other people make decisions for us. Drifting can occur any time during a person's life, but it seems to be more common when a person is young or insecure. I drifted into an accounting major because the classes were easy and my advisers said I would always be able to get a job. When I graduated, I interviewed for one job and accepted it without exploring other options. I drifted into marriage with my first serious boyfriend and although I love my husband dearly, I didn't put as much thought into the decision as I should have.

In many ways, your feelings about your possessions and situations can tell you more about yourself than the items themselves. Do you feel pride, hate, or neutrality towards your possessions/situations? Additionally, your perception of other's feelings about your possessions can be a good barometer of how much control you give to other people in your life. Remember, the more time and energy you spend worrying about other people's opinions is less time and energy you have to spend making changes in your life.

The following exercise will help you assess how you feel about your possessions and how you think other people view your outer persona.

Record the following on the worksheet.

Item: I've filled some of these in for you. Please add as many as you feel are relevant. Items can include physical items as well as situations such as your marriage/family situation and your religion.

Description: Describe the item in as much or little detail you feel is important. Include superlatives as well as straight descriptions.

How Acquired? Describe how this item came into your life. Did you drift into a decision or did you make a conscious choice?

Your feelings: Record how you feel about this item. This can be positive, negative, or neutral.

Others' Feelings: You can either ask people how they feel about your possessions or make your own assumptions. In many instances, your assumptions will tell you more than their feelings because chances are other people are less concerned about your possessions than you think they are.

Your Reaction: Are you amused, angry, or indifferent? Your reaction will gauge how much control you give other people in your life.

Will you change? Record whether or not you want to change and the reason for your decision.

Exercise-Outer Images

Item	Description	How acquired?	Your feelings
Car	*1984 blue Nissan Sentra with almost 150K miles. She has dents and dings but a wonderful personality and she always gets us where we need to be.*	*John and I both went car shopping and she was the one that we could afford and we got a good feeling from.*	*I love Kobe. She is very dependable and reliable. I get the feeling that she is taking care of us. I also feel good knowing that Kobe is paid for.*
Car			
House			
Marriage			
Children			

Exercise-Outer Images - What you are?

Item	Others' feelings	Your reaction	Will you change and why?
Car	*Other people probably think that I drive an older car because I can't afford another car.*	*I don't really care. I know why I drive my car and she's paid for.*	*No. I will keep Kobe as long as possible. She is a great car.*
Car			
House			
Marriage			
Children			

Item	Description	How acquired?	Your feelings
Religion			
Education			
Job			
Savings			
Travel Experience			

Item	Others' feelings	Your reaction	Will you change and why?
Religion			
Education			
Job			
Savings			
Travel Experience			

Item	Description	How acquired?	Your feelings
Stereo			
TV			

Item	Others' feelings	Your reaction	Will you change and why?
Stereo			
TV			

Item	Description	How acquired?	Your feelings

Item	Others' feelings	Your reaction	Will you change and why?

Analysis

In reviewing the responses you've given for each of these categories, determine if when response was Positive(P), Neutral(0) or Negative (N). You can do this by looking at your choice of words and/or analyzing your gut feeling toward this object.

When you've assessed each response, count the number of P, O, and N's across for each item and down for each column and record the counts on the following worksheet. Add your positive and neutral responses and compare the total to your negative numbers.

If the sum of your positives and neutrals is more than your negatives, your mental attitude is probably pretty good. The reverse indicates you may need to improve your mental attitude in order to make real and lasting changes in your life. I'm not Pollyanna; I don't believe in shouting with glee when you're living in the gutter. However, research has shown that a positive mental attitude allows us to see our problems realistically and take action to improve our lot in life. The "poor me" trap is hard to break out of and the energy spent waiting for a white knight to speed to the rescue would be better spent planning your escape.

Pay particular attention to your reaction to other people's feelings about your possessions. Although we all like to be liked and well thought of, sometimes in order to truly grow, it's important to pay more attention to your thoughts and feelings about your lot in life than to other people's.

Section 1- Analysis by Item					
ITEM	P	O	P+O	N	NOTES
CAR					
HOUSE					
MARRIAGE					
CHILDREN					
RELIGION					
EDUCATION					
JOB					
SAVINGS					
TRAVEL EXPERIENCE					
STEREO					
TV					
TOTALS					

Attitude Builder

Make a list of ten things you are happy about. Make copies to keep in your desk, your dresser, your bathroom and any place you may need a lift.

Section 2- Analysis by Category					
Category	**P**	**O**	**P+O**	**N**	**Notes**
Description					
How Acquired					
Your Feelings					
Others' Feelings					
Your reaction					
Will You Change					
TOTALS					

On the lines below, record your thoughts and feelings about your outer images. Are you accepting of your possessions or do you constantly feel ashamed of what you possess and the image you show the world?

Image Builder

Select one item you feel negatively about and identify one positive aspect to that item. For instance, my car is several years old and unsightly but I don't have a monthly car payment. You may not be able to identify something positive about every item on the list but there are positives to some of those seemingly negative situations. The key is to look at your negatives in a new light.

Self Description

We all live with a physical partner that we may or may not love: our bodies. Our bodies are our partners for life. Sometimes our bodies delight us, other times they disgust us. How we feel about our bodies is a good indicator of our self esteem. We can love our bodies, we can hate our bodies, or we can view them with cool, clinical detachment. Many women with model thin figures concentrate on their figure flaws because they don't really like themselves a whole lot, but other women, with larger bodies, are more accepting towards their physical beings.

In the space below, describe your physical body. Describe your height, your weight, your hair color, and anything else that you feel is important.

Review what you've written and look for buzzwords. Did you describe yourself as bountiful, fat, or obese? Are you tall, a beanpole, or gangly? Do these words have positive, negative, or neutral connotations? An abundance of negative words may mean you have a poor self image. Think about it.

Image Builder

Stand naked in front of the mirror and gaze into your eyes. What color are they? Do you like the color? Why or why not? Search your body in the mirror until you find three things you like. It can be your eyes, your hands, your dimples, your stomach, legs, feet, anything. You *have* to find three things you like. From now on when you start degrading your body remember those three things. Write them on a Post-It to stick in your calendar or in another place where you will see them on a regular basis.

Likes and Dislikes

As a human being, there are certain traits you will admire about yourself and others you detest. In the following columns, record ten things you like about yourself and ten things you dislike. These can be physical (your beautiful brown hair), personal (your compassionate spirit), or accomplishments (winning the spelling bee in 5th grade). List anything. The only rules are that you have to have at least ten of each and you have to have an equal number of likes and dislikes.

Likes	Dislikes

Was it harder to come up with likes than dislikes? That's normal, because many of us have been taught that pride is one of the "seven deadly sins." Therefore, self-depreciation is viewed as normal and healthy and self-praise is viewed as vain. After 30 years spent putting myself down, I've come to realize that a certain amount of pride is good for our self-esteem, because, after all, if we don't toot our own horns, who will? The trick is to balance "shameless self-promotion" with a sprinkling of humility.

Image Builder

Watch what you say and think. For the next week, monitor your thoughts and words. When you catch yourself putting yourself down either verbally or mentally, mentally apologize to yourself and remind yourself of your positive traits. Conversely, make a note of when you compliment yourself. If it helps, keep a short journal of all these occurrences. After a week, note how many times you have given yourself a put-down and how many times you've patted yourself on the back. Did you put yourself down more than you built yourself up? If you don't view yourself as a valuable, worthwhile person, how can you expect anyone else to?

Passions, Talents, and Skills

A popular book proclaims that if we do what we love the money will follow. In a sense, that may be true, because a vocation built around our passions will be a job we enjoy doing and we'll put more effort into it than a job we feel forced into. There is nothing more fulfilling than spending your working day doing something you love. Conversely, the day drags when filled with monotonous brainless tasks.

We don't have to give up our day jobs to incorporate our passions. I know someone who works as a grade school principal by day and indulges his passion for guitar by playing at night and on the weekends. Building a career around your interests is not for everyone, but everyone can find ways to indulge themselves and include their passions in their daily lives.

The following exercises are designed to identify your passions, talents, and skills and to help you determine where they collide and how that information can be used to your advantage.

The exercises in this section are:

Passions:	What do you love doing and why?
Talents:	What are you naturally good at, do you enjoy it and do you want to incorporate it into your life?
Skills:	What talents have you honed into skills? What skills have you developed through hard work, even though you have next to no natural ability? What skills have you developed due to necessity?
Collision of Passions/ Talents/ Skills:	This exercise identifies where your passions, talents, and skills come together and how you feel about developing these into full-time employment or how you can incorporate them Into your life.
Skills I need:	A place to record skills you'd like to develop to feed your passions.

Passions

Identify the passions in your life: the things you truly enjoy doing. These are the things that make the days race by and your heart sing.

Record the following information:

Passion: How do you describe your passion? Common passions include writing, music, spending time with your family, travel, teaching, etc. I define a passion as anything you can totally lose yourself in.

Why do you love it? What do you love about this activity? For example, I love writing because I love the flow of words and the feeling of seeing my thoughts succinctly expressed on paper. My husband loves music because it carries him to another place.

Why is this a passion? Why do you define this as a passion? Is it something you can't live without, something you feel empty if you aren't doing? Why do you believe it is a passion in your life?

Major Incorporation: How can you incorporate this passion into your life in a major way? If you love to sing, can you go on Broadway and perform? This is the time to dream. Don't let reality stop you from recording things that seem impossible.

Minor Incorporation: How can you keep your day job and incorporate your passion into your life? For instance, if singing is your passion, can you sing one night a week in a Karaoke bar, can you join a weekend band, can you join the choir at church?

As an example, I've written about my passion for writing.

Exercise—Passions

Passion	What in particular do you love?	Why is this a passion?
Writing	*The way it feels when my words flow across the page and how wonderful it is to create my own fictional universe.*	*Because I could not imagine life without writing.*

Passion	Major Incorporation	Minor Incorporation
Writing	*Quit my job and become a full-time novelist.*	*Write for smaller publications.*

Passion	What in particular do you love?	Why is this a passion?

Passion	Major Incorporation	Minor Incorporation

Analysis

By working through this exercise, you will have a better idea of what activities you are truly passionate about and will get some ideas on how to incorporate them into your life. Highlight some of the minor incorporations and start doing them. Start singing in the church choir, try out for a community theater production, or take a class in something that you love but haven't had the time to pursue. Don't give up on pursuing your dreams full time, but don't delay giving yourself joy until the kids are raised, the house is paid for, or any other reason. Many people find that once they start incorporating their passions into everyday life, they are happy and fulfilled and no longer feel the need to completely alter their life to pursue their passion.

Image Builder

Start acting like you are already doing what you love. In your free time dress the part, buy some tools of the trade, or take a class. Do anything that you can to convince yourself that you can do what you want. Once you start seeing yourself in that role, it will be easier to make your dreams come true.

Acting the part will make it easier for you to begin acting on your minor incorporations. Thinking of yourself as a singer will make it easier to go to "open mike night." Thinking of yourself as a writer will make it easier to send off your freelance articles. When I decided that I wanted to pursue my love of writing, I bought a book bag that looked as if it could belong to a bohemian writer. Carrying that helped me think of myself as a writer and I began sending articles in for publication.

Talents

We all have things we are naturally good at. Some of these talents we embrace and others we try to hide. For instance, I'm naturally good with numbers and got straight A's in all of those damned accounting classes. I mastered the concepts and skills easily; however, that talent is not one I like to use. I quit a job because my boss asked me to develop a cost of quality system and utilize my accounting background. That wasn't something that appealed to me and I didn't want to spend a year working on something I hated.

To evaluate your talents record the following:

Talent: What are you naturally good at? This can be anything from pitching a baseball to writing poems. Remember to record all your talents, not just those you enjoy doing.

Your Feelings: Sing the praises of your natural born talent or take a moment to curse your parents for passing it along to you.

Desire to incorporate into your life: If you are good at math and numbers come easily but you hate accounting and other numbers related fields, obviously you don't want to incorporate this in your life. Be honest and don't worry about whose feelings you'll hurt if you decide to check your talent at the door.

Explanation: Explain why you do or do not want to incorporate this talent into your life or why you wish you hadn't been born with this natural ability.

Method of incorporation: If you answered that you did want to incorporate this talent into your life, brainstorm and determine how to incorporate this into your life.

Exercise—Talents

Talent	Your Feeling?	Desire to incorporate in your life
Accounting skills	*I hate accounting.*	*None*

Talent	Explanation	Method of Incorporation
Accounting	*Accounting is so dull and boring because it is always the same old thing.*	*N/A*

Talent	Your Feeling?	Desire to incorporate in your life

Talent	Explanation	Method of Incorporation

Analysis

This exercise should have given you a good idea of what talents you possess that you want to incorporate into your life. Don't feel guilty about the ones you don't want to include in your lifestyle. Sometimes, the things we are born knowing how to do are not the things that interest us the most. If we pursue a god-given talent just because we are good at it, we may end up miserable.

Image Builder

Identify one talent that you have and enjoy but don't get as much time to engage in as you would like. Set aside one afternoon and spend it enjoying your talent. If you are good at writing, spend an afternoon writing. If you are a singer, spend time singing. Put yourself first and let yourself do what you are good at and enjoy.

Skills

We all have developed certain skills throughout our lifetimes, some skills because of a passion to learn and others because of circumstances. Not many people enjoy ironing but a lot of people are skilled at it because it was either learn to iron or wear wrinkled clothes. Analyzing our skills and determining which ones we want to incorporate in our lives places us one step closer to the changes we desire in our lives.

To complete the following worksheet record the following:

Skills: What skills have you developed during your life? These can include practical skills such as budgeting, fun skills such as photography or anything else you feel is a skill.

Your Feelings: Do your skills excite you, bore you, or make you wish you had taken a different path in life?

Desire to incorporate into your life? If you are good at math and numbers come easily and you've honed your accounting skills but don't want to look at another balance sheet, write it down. Don't worry. Your boss won't see this.

Why or why not? Explain why you want to incorporate this skill into your life or why you wish you hadn't developed this skill.

Method of incorporation: If you answered that you did want to incorporate this skill into your life, brainstorm and determine how you can incorporate it into your life.

Exercise—Skills

Skill	Your Feeling?	Desire to incorporate in your life
Surviving on very little money.	*I'm proud of what John and I have been able to accomplish with next to no cash.*	*I do want to have a lot more money in my life, but I plan to always be frugal.*

Skill	Why or why not?	Method of Incorporation
Surviving on very little money.	*I see so many people wasting money and my feeling is that even if you have it, you should still be frugal.*	*Continue as I'm doing and, hopefully, keep the same mindset after The Portable Coach becomes a bestseller.*

Skill	Your Feeling?	Desire to incorporate in your life

Skill	Why or Why Not?	Method of Incorporation

Analysis

From completing this exercise, you should have a good idea of what skills you possess that you want to incorporate into your life. Don't feel guilty about the ones that you want to abandon. Sometimes we have skills that we've spent years developing only to realize that they don't feed our passions or our souls. Learn to let things go. Don't worry about disappointing anyone. One definition of a wasted life is one spent in the pursuit of unhappiness. In other words, spending your life doing something you dislike will make you unhappy.

Image Builder

Practice declining requests to utilize your skills. Identify a skill that you don't enjoy but is not critical to the well being of your family or job and when someone asks you to utilize that skill, politely decline and tell them that you don't feel comfortable doing that anymore.

Just Say No

On the lines below record how you imagine people will respond when you begin to decline requests. Write down how you will respond to these individuals. This way you will be prepared when people react in shock to your declining their requests.

____

____

____

____

____

____

____

____

____

____

Where Worlds Collide

The collision of your Passions, Talents, and Skills should give you an idea where you want to go with your life. For this exercise you are only going to record the talents and skills that are related to your passion. In addition, you only want to record the skills you already possess. After this exercise is another worksheet where we'll record skills related to your passion that you need/want to acquire.

For each passion record the following:

Passions:	Describe your passion in as much detail as possible.
Talents:	List talents that are complementary to the passions. There may be more than one for each passion. Don't feel obligated to record every talent you possess.
Skills:	Record the skills that you have developed that relate to your passions.
Feelings about Passions/Talents/ Skills:	Can you put your skills and talents to work for you to do something you love? Record your thoughts on the marketability of your personal "collisions" and how you can incorporate each into your life.

Exercise—Collisions

Passion	Talents	Skills
Writing	*Imagination*	*Typing*
	Ability to plot stories	
	Organizational Skills	

Passion	Feelings
Writing	*I will continue to build on my writing talents and incorporate my passion for the written word into my life.*

Passion	Talents	Skills

Passion	Feelings

Collision Analysis

Performing this analysis should have given you an idea of what Talents and Skills are directly related to your Passions. It may have also given you an idea of what things you love, but aren't really good at. Don't worry if you don't have all the skills you need to begin fulfilling your passions, in just a minute we'll analyze what skills you need to live the life of your dreams.

Pull out your highlighter and begin to highlight those collisions that you'd like to incorporate into your life. Make sure to keep your notes in a handy place, because you'll need this information later as you begin to map out your life path.

Image Builder

Identify one collision that you can begin implementing on a small scale in your life and begin taking action to implement it. Begin writing one day a week, or sing in the shower. Whatever you can do to bring your passion into your life, start doing it now!

Skills To Develop

The preceding exercises have shown what skills you already possess that can feed your passion. Take a few more minutes to record what skills you would like to develop to more fully fuel your passion. For instance, I love to write, but my grammar doesn't always flow as smoothly as it should so I signed up for a grammar class to make me a better writer.

Jot down the following on the provided worksheet:

Passion: Identify the passion you want to feed.

Needed Skills: What skills would help you to better pursue this passion?

How to obtain: How can you obtain these skills? Can you take a class, buy a book or find a mentor?

Exercise—Needed Skills

Passion	Needed skills	How to Obtain
Writing	*Grammar*	*Take a class*
	Editing skills	

Passion	Needed skills	How to Obtain

Image Builder

Highlight the skills that are easily obtainable and take action to obtain that skill. Find someone to teach you, rent a video, or read a book. Start taking action to obtain the skills you need to fulfill your passion.

Priorities

We've all heard the phrase about "Getting our priorities straight." How many people actually sit down and get those priorities straight? I was originally going to write about values but I could never get that written. I'd stare at the computer screen awaiting a flash of brilliance that never came. Finally, I realized what I wanted to write about wasn't values but priorities. A value can be a priority: It can be important for you to be honest. But a priority such as spending more time with your family isn't one value: It can encompass several.

Using the worksheet on the following page, list your priorities in each of these categories: Family, Personal, Material, Spiritual, and Outer (World Issues). List as many as you want and don't worry about ranking them just yet.

Following are examples of some priorities in each of these areas:

Family	Personal	Material	Spiritual	Outer
Spending time with my family	Being an honest person	A safe house	Spending time in meditation	Leaving a good world for the kids
Being married	Having caring friends I can depend on	A reliable car	Going to church	No one going hungry
Taking vacations with my family	Being a good friend	A new stereo	Reading spiritual books	A safe world
Having a safe home for my kids	Being a hard worker	Planning for my future	Making time for myself	Keeping the environment clean
Putting my kids through college	Keep learning	A new computer	Living the spiritual life I choose	Fighting disease
Being accepting of my spouse	Having time to myself	A new TV	Being true to myself	
	Keeping myself in shape		Yoga	

Exercise — Priorities

Family	Personal	Material/ Professional	Spiritual	Outer

Now that you have created a list of your priorities by category, review the list and determine your top ten priorities. Unfortunately, sometimes your priorities will conflict and you'll have to rank one above the other. For instance, it would be next to impossible to train to climb Mt. Everest and have a baby in the same year. Take some time with this list, because it will come in handy when you develop your goals list in the next chapter.

1. ______________________________

2. ______________________________

3. ______________________________

4. ______________________________

5. ______________________________

6. ______________________________

7. ______________________________

8. ______________________________

9. ______________________________

10. ______________________________

Something To Think About

Do your priorities as written reflect the way you are really living your life? If family ranks above career but you spend 80 hours a week building your career, it's time to make changes. I realize that having a job is an important part of providing for your family, but can you scale it back and still provide for your family? Record your thoughts below.

A Time For Joy

This is the only life you have to live: Shouldn't it be filled with joy and happiness? Sometimes we get so caught up in the getting that we don't enjoy the having. The saddest stories I've ever read are of people who have lived their whole lives consumed with obtaining more possessions without pausing to enjoy the ones they have. Think about the uncomplicated joy of a child. We've all heard the anecdote about the child who spent more time playing with the box than the toy on Christmas morning. Children are born knowing how to find joy in the ordinary; we instill the desire for "more, more, more" into our children. They are born knowing how to find joy in the everyday.

When was the last time you smelled a flower, watched a sunset, or cuddled with your child? If you're reading this, it's not too late to bring more joy into your life. In the next few days, make an effort to enjoy the beauty of your world. You'll find that happiness and contentment breed gratitude. It is a happy paradox that being grateful for what you have will bring more abundance and joy to you.

If you're having problems finding things to be joyful for in life, take some time each evening and write down five things you are grateful for. They can be small things, such as seeing a rainbow, or big things, like seeing your first child born. The more you take time to find things to be grateful for, the happier you are likely to be.

Assignment - Joy

On the following page, record ways you can bring more joy into your life. Give yourself a deadline to accomplish each Joy!! Joys can include taking your family to the zoo, taking a walk, really watching your children playing, or listening to some good music.

Assignment Joy

Joy	Deadline

Record how it felt to take time out for joy.

Fears

Franklin D. Roosevelt once said, "We have nothing to fear but fear itself." I've learned that the unknown is much more frightening than the known. Think about a trip to the dentist; most people spent more time dreading the pain than actually feeling it. I found that once I'm able to put a name to my fears, they aren't so terrifying. An IRS audit will never be pleasant but the fear you feel may very well be worse than the audit itself. This exercise will help you name and face your fears. You'll learn to separate the fears that help you avoid real danger from those imagined fears that are hindering your progress. Once you define your fears and determine how they have helped you or hurt you it will be easier to overcome those that are standing in your way.

Record the following on the worksheet:

What are you afraid of? Define your fears in your own words. Write your fears out in as much detail as you like. Some typical fears are fear of heights, fear of poverty, and fear of death.

Why? Why are you afraid? Is this fear irrational? Dig deep into your soul and determine why you are afraid of this.

Has this helped you and how? Some fears can be healthy. A fear of dying in a car wreck may have convinced you not to ride with a drunk driver. If your fear has helped you, how?

Has this hurt you and how? What have been the negative consequences of this fear? Have you lost a job because you are afraid of failing and wouldn't take on additional responsibilities? Have you not gotten a promotion because of this fear?

Name an action you can take to overcome a fear: For fears that have hurt you in the past, give a brief statement of an action you can take to overcome your fear. For instance, if you are afraid of being broke, start saving money to have a nest egg.

Exercise—Fear

What are you afraid of?	Why?	Has this helped you and how?

What are you afraid of?	Has this hurt you and how?	Action to overcome?

What are you afraid of?	Why?	Has this helped you and how?

What are you afraid of?	Has this hurt you and how?	Action to overcome?

Analysis

Review your fears. Are they less scary now that you see them written down on paper? Have you identified actions to take to overcome the harmful fears? When I started staring fear in the face instead of running away, I found myself taking more risks and living life more fully. My writing has always had a special place in my heart and I was afraid of being rejected by editors and told that "I wasn't good enough." When I realized that this fear was holding me back, I began sending in submissions to smaller magazines and newspapers. The rejection letters weren't as painful as I feared and the first time I saw my name in print in a "real" publication I was elated. If I had continued to live in fear of rejection, I would have never known the joy of seeing my name in print. I was afraid to submit books for publication because of my fear that they would end up in the clearance rack at the bookstore along with all of the other unwanted books. Finally, I realized that it would be better to end up on the clearance rack than for my book to languish in my desk drawer.

Fear Buster

Put check marks by the small actions you can do to alleviate your fears. Begin taking action. The longest journey begins with just one step. Take that step now!

Emotions

Our methods of expressing emotions have a lot to do with our upbringing and comfort level. I used to believe that because emotions came naturally they weren't something to be controlled. My emotional style was to let it all hang out. I believed anything else was phony. I've since learned that there are better ways to express emotion than to wear your heart on your sleeve 24 hours a day. Having a poker face has its merits. I've learned to clench my fists at times or to just smile and take it. I'm currently working in a support position and the people I work with think nothing of interrupting my projects with their petty requests. I find it incredibly rude and annoying but because I still need the paycheck I do what is asked of me and then vent to my confidantes.

Self-control and self-discipline are very important skills that I've stopped looking at as being phony. They are coping mechanisms, a way of tailoring our emotions to the setting we're in. Total emotional suppression is unhealthy as well. Research has shown that suppressed emotions can manifest in physical symptoms. The key is to reach the balance between expressing and suppressing. The following exercises will give you some guidance on emotional control.

Emotional Style

Describe your emotional style. Are you cool as a cucumber, hot as a firecracker, short tempered, etc. In the space below, write as detailed a description of your emotional style as you can.

The words you chose to describe yourself will give you a clue as to whether you express or suppress your emotions. After you've described yourself, ask someone you trust to analyze your emotional style. You may find that they view you much differently than you view yourself. Discuss the differences and determine what they feel you could do differently and what they feel you are doing right. Analyze their suggestions and, if you feel there is something to them, take action. However, remember that their perception is just that: a perception that may or may not be correct. Only you know the truth. Act on suggestions you feel are relevant and store the rest in your mental filing cabinet or place them into your mental wastebasket if appropriate.

Emotional Expression

How we express our emotions tells us a great deal about our emotional style. For the next exercise complete the following:

Emotion:	I've listed some common emotions, please feel free to add any other emotions you feel are important.
When would you express this emotion?	Give an example of when you would feel this way. For instance, would you express joy when a child was born, when you see a sunset?
Where would you express this emotion?	Would you express it at home, in a business setting, or where?
Who would you feel comfortable expressing this emotion around?	Your friends, your family, who?
How would you express this emotion?	Would you cry, would you frown, would you pound your fist? Record how you would express this emotion.
Why would you express this emotion this way?	Briefly tell why. Because you feel comfortable in this setting around these people or what?

Exercise—Emotional Expression

Emotion	When would you express this emotion (example)?	Where you would express this emotion?	Who would you feel comfortable expressing this emotion around?
Anger			
Sadness			
Joy			
Fear			
Loathing			
Disgust			
Envy			
Happiness			

Emotion	How would you express this emotion?	Why would you express this emotion this way in this situation?
Anger		
Sadness		
Joy		
Fear		
Loathing		
Disgust		
Envy		
Happiness		

Emotion	When would you express this emotion (example)?	Where you would express this emotion?	Who would you feel comfortable expressing this emotion around?

Emotion	How would you express this emotion?	Why would you express this emotion this way in this situation?

Analysis

By reviewing this exercise you may be able to identify some instances where lack of emotional control has hurt you or others. For instance, if you express rage by beating your spouse or yelling at your kids, counseling may be appropriate. Appropriate ways of expressing our emotions don't harm ourselves or others and allow us to truly feel our emotions.

As with most of the exercises in this workbook, you are the only person who can truly decide if your lack of emotional control has hurt you. Be honest with yourself and record your analysis of your emotions in the summary section of this chapter.

Image Builder

From the previous exercise, identify one or more emotions you have trouble controlling. Identify the physical and mental clues that you are getting ready to express this emotion inappropriately. From now on, when you begin to feel these symptoms take deep breaths and excuse yourself if necessary. Take steps to control your emotions.

Emotion	Physical/Emotional Signs	Control Efforts

Emotional Suppression

How we suppress our emotions also tells us a great deal about our emotional style.

Emotion:	I've listed some common emotions, add any emotions you feel are important.
When would you suppress this emotion?	Give an example of when you would suppress this emotion. For instance, the rage you feel when a subordinate screws up.
Where would you suppress this emotion?	Would you suppress it at home, in a business setting or where?
Who would you feel comfortable suppressing this emotion around?	Your friends, your family, who?
How would you suppress this emotion?	Would you bite your lip, clench your fist, drink too much alcohol?
Why would you suppress this emotion this way?	Would expressing this emotion cause you to lose your job, your family, etc.?

Exercise—Emotional Suppression

Emotion	When would you suppress this emotion (example)?	Where you would suppress this emotion?	Who would you feel comfortable suppressing this emotion around?
Anger			
Sadness			
Joy			
Fear			
Loathing			
Disgust			
Envy			
Happiness			

Emotion	How would you suppress this emotion?	Why would you suppress this emotion this way in this situation?
Anger		
Sadness		
Joy		
Fear		
Loathing		
Disgust		
Envy		
Happiness		

Emotion	When would you suppress this emotion (example)?	Where you would suppress this emotion?	Who would you feel comfortable suppressing this emotion around?

Emotion	How would you suppress this emotion?	Why would you suppress this emotion this way in this situation?

Analysis

By reviewing this exercise you may be able to identify some instances where suppressing your emotions has hurt you or another. For instance, if you suppress rage by drinking too much, maybe you need to get some counseling. Appropriate ways of suppressing our emotions don't harm ourselves or others, and allow us to truly feel our emotions.

As with most of the exercises in this workbook, you are the only person who can truly decide if suppressing your emotions has hurt you. Be honest with yourself and record your analysis of your emotions in the summary section of this chapter. I caution you not to ping-pong between expression and suppression. Beating your spouse is as harmful as suppressing your emotions through alcohol. Take action to find a healthy medium.

Image Builder

From the above exercise, identify one or more emotions you suppress in a harmful way. Identify the physical and mental clues that you are getting ready to suppress this emotion and identify a better way to control or even express this emotion.

Emotion	Physical/ Emotional Signs	Expression Efforts

False Jealousy

Many people are unfamiliar with the concept of False Jealousy. When I began analyzing my life and trying to make positive life changes, I realized I spent a lot of time being jealous of people's possessions that they had acquired by making sacrifices I wasn't willing to make or in ways that I couldn't. I'm not willing to sacrifice time with my family to make more money and I don't have rich relatives who will leave me a million dollars, so spending time being jealous of friends who do have rich relatives or who are willing to work 80 hours a week is not productive. I wasted a lot of time and energy before I figured this out. To accomplish this exercise, record the following: (I've included an example to help you).

Who are you jealous of?	Remember, no one will see this but you. Now is the time to name names. Dig deep and get out all of your jealousy and the accompanying anger.
Why or what?	What do they have that you want? A new sports car? A perfect figure? Write it down.
How did they acquire this?	What sacrifices did they make? Do they work 80 hours a week, did their grandparents leave them money? If you don't know, it's okay to put that but try to figure it out if you can.
How can you acquire this?	Can you acquire it by making the same sacrifices they did or by making other sacrifices? Write down how you think you can get this item.
Are you willing?	Are you willing to do what it takes to get this item? Don't be ashamed of saying no. Through a process of elimination, we sometimes determine what sacrifices we aren't willing to make.

Exercise—False Jealousy

Who are you jealous of?	Why or what	How did they acquire this? What sacrifices did they make?
My friend Sam	*He makes $100K a year and drives a great car*	*He works 75 hours a week and is always on call to the company. He sold his soul.*

Who are you jealous of?	How can you acquire this?	Are you willing?
My friend Sam	*By working the same number of hours and spending time away from my family*	*No*

Who are you jealous of?	Why or what	How did they acquire this? What sacrifices did they make?

Who are you jealous of?	How can you acquire this?	Are you willing?

Analysis

Hopefully, this exercise helped you to put things in a more realistic perspective. By analyzing what other people have and how they got it, it is easier to determine if your jealousy is justified or if you should let it go. Highlight all the things that you answered you are willing to work for. These will be recorded on our summary sheet at the end of the chapter.

Image Builder

Begin taking action to acquire some of the things on your list. Make those sacrifices you are willing to make and give yourself permission to have nice things. Do something for yourself. I've found that being nice to myself is one of the surest ways for me to think about what I do have and quit worrying about what I don't.

Risk Taking

To some, the security of a weekly paycheck is worth the sacrifice of leisure time and dreams. They like knowing their bills will always be paid, even if it means working at a monotonous job for forty years until retirement. To others, being stuck in one place for forty years is a vision of hell itself. They would rather risk being homeless and penniless than accept the “prison” a steady paycheck represents.

The following three scenarios are designed to analyze whether you are a fearless risk taker, a calculated risk taker, or a security craver. There is no right or wrong answer and there is nothing wrong with any of the three styles. There are trade offs. I believe you can never experience the dizzying highs if you aren’t willing to experience the lows. Others prefer a middle course and some people feel safest staying in familiar settings and situations.

I’m a risk taker and I’ve done things in my life that security cravers consider stupid. I hate regular jobs and get claustrophobic when I’m at a job for more than 18 months. I like climbing the next mountain to see what’s on the other side. However, I’ve learned to balance this risk taking with the security of my family. They fulfill my need for security and I’m free to take all the risks I want in job scenarios. My only rule is that my children are always fed and the gas and lights stay connected.

Read the following scenarios and determine which appeals to you. None of them may be an exact match for your dreams but one of them should be close to your comfort zone.

Background

You graduated from college 10 years ago and landed a job as a marketing trainee for a Fortune 500 company. The company is large and very political. In order to do well at your job, you have to conform to both the written and unwritten company policies. You feel as if you are under scrutiny 24 hours a day. You've finally become a middle manager and the pressure to conform has gotten worse. Your boss has told you that riding a motorcycle and smoking don't fit the "corporate image" and if you want another promotion you should give up both. Of course, that wasn't a demand, just "friendly advice." You're married with two children and your spouse is only working part time until both children are in school full time. You have a $1,400 a month mortgage and two car payments. You are currently making $60,000 a year.

Scenario 1

You cave into your boss' demands and give up the motorcycle and cigarettes. In your desk drawer is a calendar counting days until retirement. You enjoy collecting your weekly paycheck and planning your yearly vacation to Hawaii.

Scenario 2

You analyze your financial situation and realize that if you sold your house and bought a smaller one, you could live on less. You start sending out resumes and land a job with a smaller company. It pays less money but you are given more creative freedom and the atmosphere is more laid back.

Scenario 3

You analyze your finances and realize you could sell your house and rent a nice three bedroom house, get rid of one car, and pay your bills on $30,000. You quit your job and take on temporary assignments while you work on starting your own business. You can't provide as many luxuries for your family but you feel as if you are being true to yourself and in 10 years you could be a millionaire. You relish the feeling of control that bucking the corporate system gives you.

Analysis

Scenario 1: You crave security and would rather have the guaranteed paycheck than risk failure at a new position.

Scenario 2: You are a calculated risk taker and you'll trade one job for another you believe will make you happy.

Scenario 3: You are an all out risk taker and your life will never be boring (or secure).

As I've said none of these choices is right or wrong. You are the only one who can decide what is the right course of action for you. However, if fulfilling your dreams involves taking risks and you think it's a major risk to play hooky and call in sick, you need to either rethink your dreams or increase your risk taking skills.

Image Builder

If you are a security craver who longs to be adventurous and daring, find one small risk that you can take today. Wear an outfit that "isn't you," risk being late and find a new way to work, ask someone you admire to join you for lunch. Each small risk you take will give you more courage for the next risk. Make a list of the small risks that you are willing to take on the following page.

Risks I'm Willing To Take!!

Operational Style

We all have a different style of living our lives. Some of us prefer to be in charge and explore uncharted waters and others prefer the comfort of taking orders. There's nothing wrong with either operational style, but it is important to identify your style.

If your dream is to pilot a starship but you don't have the leadership skills to chair a committee for the PTA fun fair, you may need to work on your operational style and start being more of a leader.

For each scenario, determine whether you would be more likely to select the choice in Column A or Column B and put a check mark by your selection. Then tally the number of selections for each.

Scenario	Column A	✓	Column B	✓
1. You've been asked to help with the PTA Fair. Do you feel more comfortable:	Leading a committee and soliciting volunteers or donations.		Volunteering and showing up at the assigned time, doing your stint and leaving (or not helping out at all).	
2. You've been offered two positions, paying the same. The positions are:	A position where your boss gives you a project and the freedom to carry out the project any way you see fit.		A job where your day is filled with preassigned tasks, a regular schedule, and no overtime.	
3. Your spouse suddenly departs, leaving you and your two children penniless. Do you:	Spend some time mourning, then update your resume and hit the streets looking for a job.		Sink into a deep depression and move back in with your parents.	
4. Your view of working as a receptionist:	It is mindless and demeaning. I could only do it short term if I needed the money or it provided time to accomplish other goals.		It's an interesting job. I get to learn about the company and I love talking on the phone.	
5. If you were on the Starship Enterprise would you be:	On the bridge. I love the thrill of being in middle of all the action.		A bartender in Ten-Forward. I love the thrill of space exploration but don't want to make tough decisions.	
Totals:				

Analysis

If you had more Column A answers, you are more of a leader and willingly accept the risk of failure. To you the fun is in managing the project and making decisions.

If you had more entries in Column B, you're more of a follower. You still like going places, but you don't like to risk making the wrong decision. You may enjoy working hard and have a strong work ethic but you still don't want to be in the hot seat.

Image Builder

Find one safe assignment and change roles. This should be an assignment where failure doesn't put anything important to you at risk. If you are asked to help with a special assignment and you normally chair a committee, let someone else be in charge and practice being a follower. Conversely, if you are asked to participate and you normally follow, volunteer to chair a committee or take on additional responsibilities.

This exercise will give you respect for people with different styles. If you are a leader, you may find it's nice to let someone be in charge for a while. And if you are normally a follower, you might find you're good at leading.

Self Confidence

In order to make changes in your life, you need to feel self-confident. You need to believe that you can make these changes. It may be scary, but when the chips are down, the only person you can depend on is yourself.

Lack of self-confidence doesn't make you incompetent or stupid. It's just another thing that you need to work on improving. I grew up with low self confidence. I always felt that everyone else was better than I was. I was afraid to take risks because I knew I would fail. When I turned 30 I looked at my life and counted up my string of successes versus failures and I realized that my judgment was usually good. The only regrets I had were the times when I let my negative self-talk stop me from doing things that I really wanted to try.

The following exercise will give you an idea of how self-confident you are. For each scenario, determine if your response most closely matches Column A or Column B. Although they may not be exact matches, one should be close to how you would behave in a given situation.

After you've selected a response for the scenarios, total your "A" responses and "B" responses and record them. Then analyze your results.

Self Confidence Rating

Scenario	Column A	✓	Column B	✓
1. You walk into a large party and realize that you have toilet paper stuck on your shoe. Do you:	Run to the bathroom to remove it and stay in there 1/2 hour until you feel it is safe.		Nonchalantly reach down, pull it off and continue having a good time.	
2. You've been fired from a good job because you were too vocal about your political views. Do you feel that:	You should have kept your mouth shut and that you were wrong to express your opinions.		The position wasn't a good match and you're lucky that now you can look for something that better fits your personality.	
3. You've been put in charge of an important project at work because your boss feels your work has been great and you can handle the responsibility. Do you:	Ask to be reassigned because you're sure you can't do the work, or you procrastinate so long in starting that you have no chance of doing a great job.		Dive in knowing that you can handle what comes your way and that you'll do such a wonderful job you will be the next vice president.	
4. You've been dropped into alien space and find yourself in the middle of a bar. The aliens seem to understand you. Do you:	Look for the nearest exit and leave. I mean, who knows where these aliens have been?		Try to make friends and enjoy yourself. After all, who knows how long you'll be here?	

Scenario	Column A	✓	Column B	✓
5. After having your second child, you've gained 75 pounds. Do you:	Hide in the house until you lose the weight.		Realize that there is more to you than your body and continue making friends and being sociable.	
6. Imagine you are back in grade school and the school yard bullies are taunting you. The following happens:	Tears well up in your eyes and you run to find the teacher. Or you pretend to ignore the abuse, but it makes you feel as if you were 2 inches tall and you wonder how you got to be such a lousy person.		You feel sorry for them. The only way that they can feel good about themselves is to make someone else feel bad.	
7. The local newspaper announces it will give $500 to the person with the loudest scream. Do you:	Convince yourself that you could never humiliate yourself like that. How degrading.		Go for it. You could use the money, and it sounds like fun.	
8. You just returned from a whirlwind tour of Europe and the local paper has asked you to write an article. Do you:	Procrastinate because you know that you could never write an article that would be good enough to publish.		Write it the night after you get back and glow with pride when it gets published.	

Scenario	Column A	✓	Column B	✓
9. You have a yard sale and no one buys anything, even though you have lots of lookers. Do you:	Feel personally rejected.		Blow it off. It's a nice day to sit outside.	
10. Your boss reviews a report you completed on sales figures for your region and makes a few corrections. Do you:	Only see the red and ignore his positive comments.		Thank him for his input and make the changes he's recommended, knowing that they make the report better.	
Totals:				

Analysis

The more column B's you've got, the more self confident you are. I've established the following scale to give you an idea of your self confidence quotient.

8-10: You're self confident and can handle yourself in most situations.
5-7: You're fairly self confident but certain triggers can make you cringe.
under 5: You need to work on improving your self confidence.

Image Builder

A lot of the exercises in Section 3, Taking the Plunge, will help you build your self confidence. One of the ways I've found to improve my self confidence is to give myself tests. I place myself in situations I know will make me uncomfortable and insecure and force myself to feel secure. I ensure these situations are not life, job, or family threatening, then walk in with my head held high and let the chips fall where they may. I've always been shy at public speaking but I forced myself to enter an oratory contest and I won. I've learned I can handle myself in a wide variety of situations and now the thrill of new situations excites me.

Who Are You?

We're all individuals entitled to our own triumphs, mistakes, and quirks. The one important lesson that I've learned from almost 14 years of marriage is that what makes me happy doesn't always make my husband happy. For instance, I can spend hours engrossed in the pages of a good book, but my husband would much prefer an evening spent watching sports. We've also both learned that it is important to be true to our individual styles and make time to spend doing the things we enjoy, even if it means doing them alone.

Hopefully the exercises in this section have helped you learn about yourself and identify your comfort zone. However, knowing your comfort zone does not mean that you have to always operate within it. True growth sometimes comes from pushing your limits.

Summarize the self-knowledge you've gained below and make sure to keep it handy, because you'll need it later. I always find it interesting to read through personal growth work I've done, because it gives me a little bit of insight into who I was when I answered the questions. You might find that you want to do these exercises more than once and that every time you do them, your answers change slightly. You could consider this a baby book of your personal development and every time you go through the questions again, you can chart your personal progress.

Was your analysis of your outer images positive, negative, or neutral?

____

____

Was your description of yourself positive, negative, or neutral?

____

____

How can you improve your self image?

____

____

Can you change your attitudes without changing the possessions?

____

____

____

Summarize your top three passions and their accompanying talents and skills:

Passion	Talent	Skill

Record the skills you'd like to develop to feed your passion:

Passion	Skill

List your top 10 priorities:	
1.	6.
2.	7.
3.	8.
4.	9.
5.	10.

Describe your top three harmful fears:

1. ____
2. ____
3. ____

What emotional control problems do you need to work on?

____

____

What false jealousy issues do you have?

____

____

Are you a risk taker? ____________________

What is your operational style? ____________________

How self confident are you? ____________________

Note To Yourself

Hopefully by working through these exercises, you've gained a better understanding of who you are. Take some time to think about things you've done in your life that you are proud of. Remind yourself that you are truly a unique and wonderful person.

Record your thoughts on Section 1.

The Importance of Goals

Many people drift through life. They have nebulous notions of what they want but no hard-edged written goals. I know what that's like because I drifted through the first 26 years of my life and went where the currents took me. It wasn't until I started establishing written goals and working to achieve them that I stopped drifting and started rowing my own boat.

The very act of putting your hopes and dreams into the written word forces you to define them and subconsciously prods you towards accomplishment. I haven't accomplished every goal I've written down, but I've accomplished more of the goals I committed to writing than others that I didn't have the confidence to put into writing.

I'm a free spirit and the act of planning is not my favorite pastime, but I've come to realize that unless I establish realistic, accomplishable goals and a plan of accomplishment, I will never achieve what I want to achieve.

When I first started setting goals, I came up with grandiose plans like losing 50 pounds, saving a million dollars, and writing a best-selling novel. I soon forgot these goals because they weren't realistic, they weren't definite, and some depended on other people. I did accomplish the goals of writing a book, becoming a full-time freelancer, and spending more time with my children, because these goals were realistic, definite, and depended on no one but myself.

In order for a goal to be valuable it has to:

1. ***Be accomplishable and realistic.*** It has to be something that you believe you can accomplish. If I don't believe I can save a million dollars, I won't work towards it and I won't accomplish it. I did believe I could save $10,000 and I accomplished that goal. Once I reached that goal, I set another goal. Goals are like stepping stones, you set one and reach it and then set another one and so forth.
2. ***Be definite.*** Well defined goals are easier to accomplish than nebulous "wannas." The goal of saving $10.00 a week is easier to obtain than to "save some money." How much is some? Are you reaching your goal if you save $1.00 a week or isn't that enough?

3. ***Have a defined time limit.*** Set a date by which you want to accomplish this goal. This will prod you into action and help you to accomplish your goals.
4. ***Be within your control.*** A goal of publishing a best selling novel within the year is unrealistic because you can't control whether an agent or publisher will buy your book or if the public will read it. However, you can accomplish the goal of writing a book by this time next year. It has also gotten much easier to publish a book with the advent of print-on-demand technology and e-publishing.
5. ***Be flexible***. Sometimes, goals are set with all of the above in mind and you still can't meet them. Unforeseen circumstances arise, you decide to devote time and energy to another goal, etc. Be flexible and be willing to reevaluate your goals.

This section will help you to set realistic goals and rank them according to your personal priorities. The goals you set should be in line with the values, fears, and style that you identified in Section 1. If your style is follower and you want to start your own business, you will need to take intermediate steps to improve your leadership style.

You can make positive changes in your life!!

Fantasies and Daydreams

Although many people discount the importance of fantasies and daydreams in planning a "serious life," I firmly believe that they are important tools because they can give you clues as to who you want to be and what is important in your life. When we were kids we all had daydreams about what we wanted to be when we grew up. I've had a fascination with the written word since I was small and I knew that I would never be happy unless I had a job that involved writing. So here you're reading the fulfillment of my childhood fantasy. This section will help you identify your fantasies and set goals that will help you become the person you want to be.

In this section you will be setting Personal, Spiritual, Family, Professional/Material and Outer goals. I'll explain a little more about each one in that particular section but for each of these areas I'm going to ask you to describe a favorite fantasy or daydream about that aspect of your life and then identify the Who, What, Where, Why and How for each fantasy. By describing your ideal life, you'll gain valuable insights into who you want to be when you grow up. After you've answered the questions, compile a preliminary goals list based upon your fantasies.

Personal Goals

Personal goals are those sometimes selfish goals that we have; the things we would accomplish if we were responsible to or for no one. These are the dreams of involve leaving home for six months to backpack through Europe, abandoning your family to pursue an acting career, or quitting your job to become a monk.

On the lines below, describe what you would do if you had no responsibilities, where you would be, what you would look like, etc. In this exercise, you only have to answer to yourself. There are no kids to feed or bills to pay. Your only obligation is to be happy. In this scenario, you are the only significant person. Anyone else exists to pleasure you.

Describe yourself in this daydream/fantasy. What were you wearing, what was your health, what was your physical shape, how did you feel, etc.?

Describe the people you were with. What were they wearing, who were they, how did they feel, etc.

What were you doing?

What were the people you were with doing?

Where were you at? Describe the location in as much detail as possible.

Why were you doing what you were doing? You wanted to? Someone forced you to? You felt you had to? etc.

How were you behaving? Were you acting in a decisive manner, slow, as if it were a joke, etc.

How was everyone else behaving?

When did this fantasy/daydream occur?

Review what you've written and highlight the most important phrases for each of your answers. Using this information and your answers in Section 1 record an initial list of personal goals. This is a scratch list and all of the things you list may or may not make your final goals list.

Spiritual Goals

The word spiritual has different connotations to different people. I define spiritual goals as those that let you get in touch with yourself and a higher being. Spiritual goals can include church, meditation, and yoga.

Describe how you would worship if you were given complete freedom. Would you worship in a church, alone, how?

Describe yourself in this daydream/fantasy. What were you wearing, what was your health, what was your physical shape, how did you feel, etc.?

Describe the people you were with. What were they wearing, who were they, how did they feel, etc.?

What were you doing?

What were the people you were with doing?

Where were you at? Describe the location in as much detail as possible.

Why were you doing what you were doing? You wanted to? Someone forced you to? You felt you had to? etc.

How were you behaving? Were you acting in a decisive manner, slow, as if it were a joke, etc.

How was everyone else behaving?

When did this fantasy/daydream occur?

Now go through and highlight what aspects of your answers to each of these questions were important. These and the information you recorded earlier are the basis of your goals. Record your preliminary Spiritual Goals.

Family Goals

Family goals encompass your dreams for your ideal family and/or marital status. Describe your ideal family. Is everyone kind and loving? Are you enjoying each other's company? Who do you want in your family? Don't feel guilty if your ideal doesn't match your family. This is the place to dream.

Describe yourself in this daydream/fantasy. What were you wearing, what was your health, what was your physical shape, how did you feel, etc.?

Describe the people you were with. What were they wearing, who were they, how did they feel, etc.?

What were you doing?

What were the people you were with doing?

Where were you at? Describe the location in as much detail as possible.

Why were you doing what you were doing? You wanted to? Someone forced you to? You felt you had to? etc.

How were you behaving? Were you acting in a decisive manner, slow, as if it were a joke, etc.

How was everyone else behaving?

When did this fantasy/daydream occur?

Now go through and highlight what aspects of your answers to each of these questions were important. These and the information you recorded earlier are the basis of your goals. Record your preliminary Family Goals.

Professional/Material Goals

Professional and material goals are best summed up as Money Goals! These include the perfect way to make money and the perfect possessions to spend money on. Record your childhood fantasies of what you wanted to be when you grew up and record your ideal material setting and possessions.

Describe yourself in this daydream/fantasy. What were you wearing, what was your health, what was your physical shape, how did you feel, etc.?

Describe the people you were with. What were they wearing, who were they, how did they feel, etc.?

What were you doing?

What were the people you were with doing?

Where were you at? Describe the location in as much detail as possible

Why were you doing what you were doing? You wanted to? Someone forced you to? You felt you had to? etc.

How were you behaving? Were you acting in a decisive manner, slow, as if it were a joke, etc.

How was everyone else behaving?

When did this fantasy/daydream occur?

Now go through and highlight what aspects of your answers to each of these questions were important. These and the information you recorded earlier are the basis of your goals. Record your preliminary Professional/Material Goals.

Outer Goals

These are the goals you have for the rest of the world. They can include world peace, feeding the children, saving the environment. What would you do if you could devote your time to helping others?

Describe yourself in this daydream/fantasy. What were you wearing, what was your health, what was your physical shape, how did you feel, etc.?

Describe the people you were with. What were they wearing, who were they, how did they feel, etc.?

What were you doing?

What were the people you were with doing?

Where were you at? Describe the location in as much detail as possible.

Why were you doing what you were doing? You wanted to? Someone forced you to? You felt you had to? etc.

How were you behaving? Were you acting in a decisive manner, slow, as if it were a joke, etc.

How was everyone else behaving?

When did this fantasy/daydream occur?

Now go through and highlight what aspects of your answers to each of these questions were important. These and the information you recorded earlier are the basis of your goals. Record your Outer Goals.

Important Goals

Now that you've looked at goals in each of the above areas, it's time to rate your goals. Go through each of the above areas and rate your goals, number 1 being the most important. After you have completed this, copy your most important goals here.

Final Goals List

Now review your goals and determine whether any of them are "conflicting." Conflicting goals are those that cannot be accomplished at the same time due to limited time and/or resources. An example of conflicting goals would be having a child within a year and spending the next year backpacking in Europe. It would be difficult to accomplish both of them at once. If you have any conflicting goals, highlight them and prioritize them as to which you wish to accomplish first. Using the list above and your notes about conflicting goals, rank your goals again with number 1 being the most important. Then copy your top 20 goals on the chart on the following page, assign a time frame for completion, and add notes as to how you can accomplish this goal.

Final Goals List

Goal	Time Frame	Notes
1.		
2.		
3.		
4.		
5.		
6.		
7.		
8.		
9.		
10.		
11.		
12.		
13.		
14.		
15.		
16.		
17.		
18.		
19.		
20.		

Now that this is accomplished, it's time to pack for your journey of self.

Skill Builder

Select a small, easily accomplished goal and do it. If your picture of ideal family life included a trip to a zoo or a museum, make the trip. If you want a new bicycle and it's within your means, buy it.

Allow yourself to dream. If you want to take a trip to the Bahamas, visit a travel agent and pick up brochures. The more real you make your dream, the easier it will be to accomplish.

Notes on Section 2

Packing

Making major life changes is like packing for a trip, but instead of socks and underwear, you'll be packing your bags with courage, a realistic financial plan, and a little love from your friends.

This section will help you do some hard-core planning for your life needs. I've found that putting a detailed plan for accomplishing my goal on paper makes it easier for me to believe it can really happen and to take action to make it happen. It is also easier to turn your goals into reality if you carefully analyze and plan for your financial and emotional needs. Working through the exercises in this section will help you build your self-esteem and a support network.

One caveat: Don't spend so much time planning for the trip that you never leave. It is easy to get trapped into overplanning and never begin working on your life. I know that it is a lot easier to plan than to do and I've known perpetual students who crave the security of academia but are terrified of being out in the world.

In this section you'll be:

- **Making a list of your Accomplishments**
- **Obtaining Letters of Reference**
- **Conducting Disaster Planning**
- **Making FishFlows to organize Your Plan of Attack**
- **Developing a Five Year Plan**
- **Analyzing the Costs of Achieving Your Goals**
- **Learning Organizational Skills**
- **Developing Emotional Skills**
- **Reviewing the Company You Keep**

Good luck on your journey of self!

Accomplishments

Change is a scary thing, even when we are going towards something we want and are excited about accomplishing. I'll be honest with you, there will be times when your self-doubt is enormous and you want to give up. One great way to counter your doubt is to create a list of all of your accomplishments that you can pull out when you're filled with self-doubt to remind yourself of all the things that have gone right in your life.

Your list of accomplishments should include all the things you've accomplished in your life that you're proud of, including that medal you won in the second grade spelling bee, your two beautiful kids, and the great new job you just landed.

On the following lines list at least ten things you are proud of. If you can't think of ten things, ask your friends and family members for help.

1. ______________________________
2. ______________________________
3. ______________________________
4. ______________________________
5. ______________________________
6. ______________________________
7. ______________________________
8. ______________________________
9. ______________________________
10. ______________________________

When you've finished your list, post it someplace where you can see it when you're feeling down. Or better yet, make several copies and stick them in your desk at work, on your refrigerator, and anyplace else where you'll see them often. By reminding yourself of your past accomplishments, it reminds you that you've done all of these great things. Surely you can accomplish your new goals as well. Whatever you do, don't tell yourself that the only reason you were able to accomplish all these things was to be in the right place at the right time. These are accomplishments you worked for and should be proud of.

Skill Builder

Next time you're feeling down, remember the wonderful feeling of accomplishment that comes from reaching a goal and let yourself imagine how wonderful you're going to feel when you reach your new goals. Imagining the success makes it more real and that much easier to accomplish.

Letters of Reference

Job seekers request letters of reference from colleagues. I've done it myself and it's wonderful to see what people who respect your work have to say about you. I take out my letters of reference occasionally and re-read them just to remind myself that I am a worthy person.

If you are seeking a job then by all means ask your colleagues for letters of reference, but also ask your friends and colleagues for letters of reference detailing all the great things you've done in your life. Ask your husband to write about why he married you, ask your daughter to write about a favorite activity the two of you have shared. One of my favorite possessions is an essay my daughter wrote for school about her favorite person: me.

Your assignment is to obtain three letters of reference containing only positive things, if someone writes something negative, rip the letter up or ask them to rewrite it. These letters of reference can include the very personal (a good cook, a wonderful parent, helps me with my homework) and more practical (very detail oriented and responsible). If one person won't give you a letter of reference then ask someone else. In the space below, keep a log of your letter of reference requests.

Name Requested From	Relationship	Response

After you've obtained your letters of reference, put them in a safe place and pull them out when you're having self doubts.

Skill Builder

Write your own reference letter on the next page. On several occasions, I've asked colleagues to write reference letters for me and they told me to just write something for them to sign. The first one was difficult to write because it felt like unabashed bragging. However, as soon as I remembered that someone else would be signing it, it was easy to wax poetic about how wonderful I am. Reacquaint yourself with your imaginary friend from childhood and have them write you a reference letter. Give yourself permission to be wonderful!

My Reference Letter

Disaster Planning

Governments hope that disasters and wars won't occur; however, our federal government has an agency devoted to disaster planning. Even though you don't want to fail at your dreams and you've spent a considerable amount of time building your self esteem as you work through this book, you live in the real world and things do go wrong. In this section you're going to act as your own FEMA and plan for your personal disaster. Let your imagination run wild and write down the very worst things that can happen if you begin making changes in your life. This can include going bankrupt or your husband leaving you. When I first began making changes in my life, I felt I would be setting myself up for failure if I even contemplated the downside of change. I've learned that writing my fears down makes them less scary and if the worst does happen I have a place to start my disaster recovery efforts.

In the worksheet below record the following:

Goal: Which goal are we talking about. Is it a new job or bicycling to Argentina?

Worst thing that can happen: List every conceivable fear from the realistic to the ridiculous.

Plausibility: How realistic is it to expect that this awful thing will happen to you? Chances are all of your friends and family aren't going to desert you. Some may have difficulty dealing with it but some may surprise you with their reaction.

How to handle it: If the worst does happen can you handle it and how? If you really cannot handle this consequence of your change, note that here and rethink your decision. You may want to back off one or more of your goals until you feel better able to handle the consequences. However, do a lot of soul searching before you decide to completely give up a goal.

Exercise—Disaster Planning

Goal	Worst Case	Plausibility	Can you and how will you deal with this reaction?
Becoming a full-time freelancer	*I won't get assignments and I'll starve to death.*	*Not very*	*I'll make sure that I have temp assignments or other sources of income lined up.*

Goal	Worst Case	Plausibility	Can you and how will you deal with this reaction?

Goal	Worst Case	Plausibility	Can you and how will you deal with this reaction?

Analysis

Many times when we name our worst fears we find they aren't as scary as we thought they would be. We also realize that some of our fears are so implausible it's amazing we convinced ourselves that these awful things could really happen. Occasionally, we name valid concerns and those are the ones we need to consider in determining whether or not to proceed with our goals.

In the following exercise you'll weigh the consequences of your worst fears against the benefit of achieving your goals.

Record the following:

Goal:	What goal does this pertain to?
Fear:	What realistic, plausible fear is holding you back from accomplishing this goal?
Benefits of pursuing goal:	What will happen if you fulfill this goal? Will your self-esteem increase? Will you get a raise?
Benefits of not pursuing goal:	If you choose to drop this goal, how will you benefit? Does staying mean you can maintain the status quo?
Decision:	What are you going to do? Record your decision. This can include alternate methods of satisfying your inner spirit. For instance, if you have a family and children it may be unrealistic to go to Hollywood to pursue an acting career. However, acting in local theater could satisfy your urge to act without uprooting your family.

I've included a sample analysis to make it easier for you to analyze your own goals.

Exercise—Weighing the Benefits

Goal	Fear	Benefit of pursuing goal
To advance my career by accepting a career in Seattle	*I'll disrupt my entire family by moving*	*I benefit from a career change and more prestige*

Goal	Benefit of not pursuing goal	Decision
To advance my career by accepting a career in Seattle	*My children are allowed to graduate from high school with their friends.*	*To stay where I'm at and look for a job locally that would satisfy my career needs.*

Goal	Fear	Benefit of pursuing goal

Goal	Benefit of not pursuing goal	Decision

Review

Hopefully, the previous exercises have helped you determine if your fears are realistic or not and determine whether the risks of pursuing your goal are worth it. We live in the real world and the real world is about compromise. I don't believe we can have it all and we need to make decisions based not only upon our lives, but also on what's best for those we love. Sometimes, we make a decision in our best interest and other times we put their interests first. I do believe that we can all have rich satisfying lives that satisfy our passions. We just need to be flexible in deciding what form this fulfillment takes. Singing in your church choir may not be as prestigious as a world tour, but it will allow you to indulge your love of singing.

Many times we make decisions based upon what we think other people, especially our families, want. We don't always ask their opinions. Sometimes, their reactions surprise and delight us. For instance, when I was offered a chance to go to Japan four months after my son was born, I was afraid my parents would be disappointed that we were taking their only grandson 10,000 miles away. They were thrilled for me and encouraged us to go. Don't make your decisions in a vacuum. Consult your loved ones.

FishFlowing

I've refined the techniques I used as I wrote this book. Originally, I flowcharted the process but my flowcharts never gave me a good picture of what I wanted to. Using a cause and effect chart such as a classic fishbone didn't properly present the process either. That's when I designed a FishFlow. It contains elements of a classic flowchart and a fishbone diagram but it is beneficial in helping to define goals.

This process can be used for any goal but is of most use in goals that involve many steps. You wouldn't use this to plan a trip to the local zoo but it would help in planning a week long vacation. The first step in FishFlowing is to break your goal into smaller steps. Most goals can be accomplished with ten main steps and then subsidiary steps. Two steps that should be part of any life changing goals are Emotional and Financial preparedness. Make sure that you are emotionally ready to begin the process and make sure that you will be able to pay your bills while you are undergoing the process. On a blank piece of paper write your goal at the top of the page, and then all the steps you need to take to reach your goal. This is a brainstorming session. Some of the steps may be minuscule and others may be gargantuan. Once you've listed every step you can possibly think of, take your trusty highlighter and highlight the larger (gargantuan) steps. Then take out pieces of paper for each of these sub goals and repeat the process, brainstorming each of these substeps into manageable steps.

Major Rule

One of my major rules for goal setting is that I should be able to accomplish or control every step within the process. For instance, if my goal is to purchase a home, I cannot control what the realtor does, but I can control the selection of a realtor.

There are two exceptions to this rule:

- ☯ **Group Goals:** If your goal is shared with your spouse or another person, it's okay to allow that person to control some of the steps. For instance, in purchasing an automobile, many wives defer to their husband's opinion of the mechanical aspects of the car.
- ☯ **Anonymous Decision Makers:** The other exception to this rule is made for sales people. It is okay to set sales goals because these goals require that people purchase from you, not that any particular individual purchases from you.

After you have your steps and sub-steps laid out, it's time to FishFlow. The box at the bottom of the page represents where you are now and the box at the top represents the accomplishment of your goal. Each of the boxes in between is a major step and the boxes above and below represent sub-steps. Between the major step and the substep is room to write the details of accomplishing the sub-step. I know it sounds confusing, but in addition to a blank chart, I've included a chart diagramming the process of completing this book. As you might note, my goal was not to sell The Portable Coach but to complete the book and present it to publishers. I could not control whether or not they purchased the book. All I could do was present it to them.

You may want to take the blank chart and blow it up to a larger size on a copy machine to give you more room to work. Feel free to add color, pictures, anything you want to make it yours.

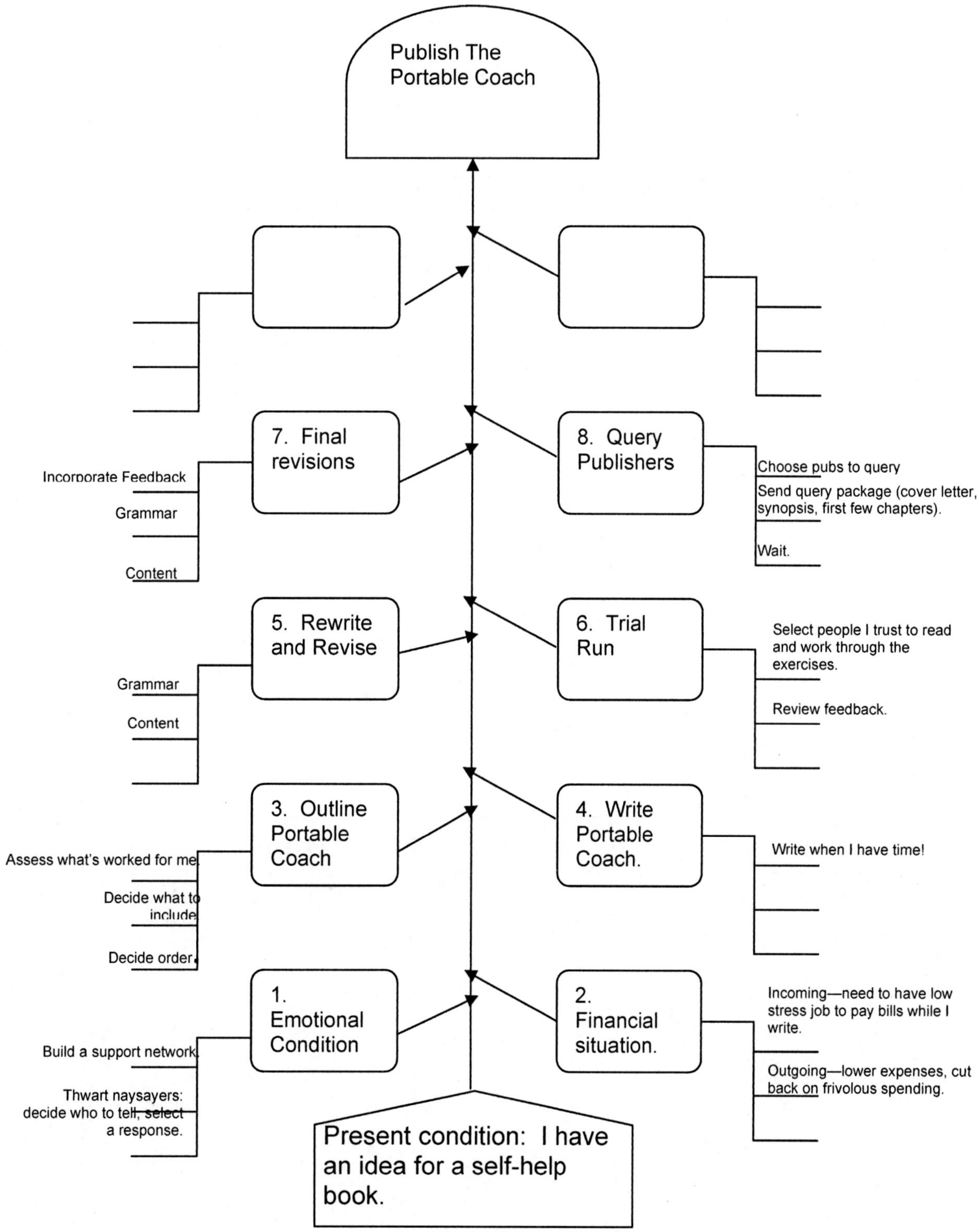
Publish The Portable Coach
7. Final revisions
Incorporate Feedback
Grammar
Content
8. Query Publishers
Choose pubs to query
Send query package (cover letter, synopsis, first few chapters).
Wait.
5. Rewrite and Revise
Grammar
Content
6. Trial Run
Select people I trust to read and work through the exercises.
Review feedback.
3. Outline Portable Coach
Assess what's worked for me
Decide what to include
Decide order.
4. Write Portable Coach.
Write when I have time!
1. Emotional Condition
Build a support network
Thwart naysayers: decide who to tell, select a response.
2. Financial situation.
Incoming—need to have low stress job to pay bills while I write.
Outgoing—lower expenses, cut back on frivolous spending.
Present condition: I have an idea for a self-help book.

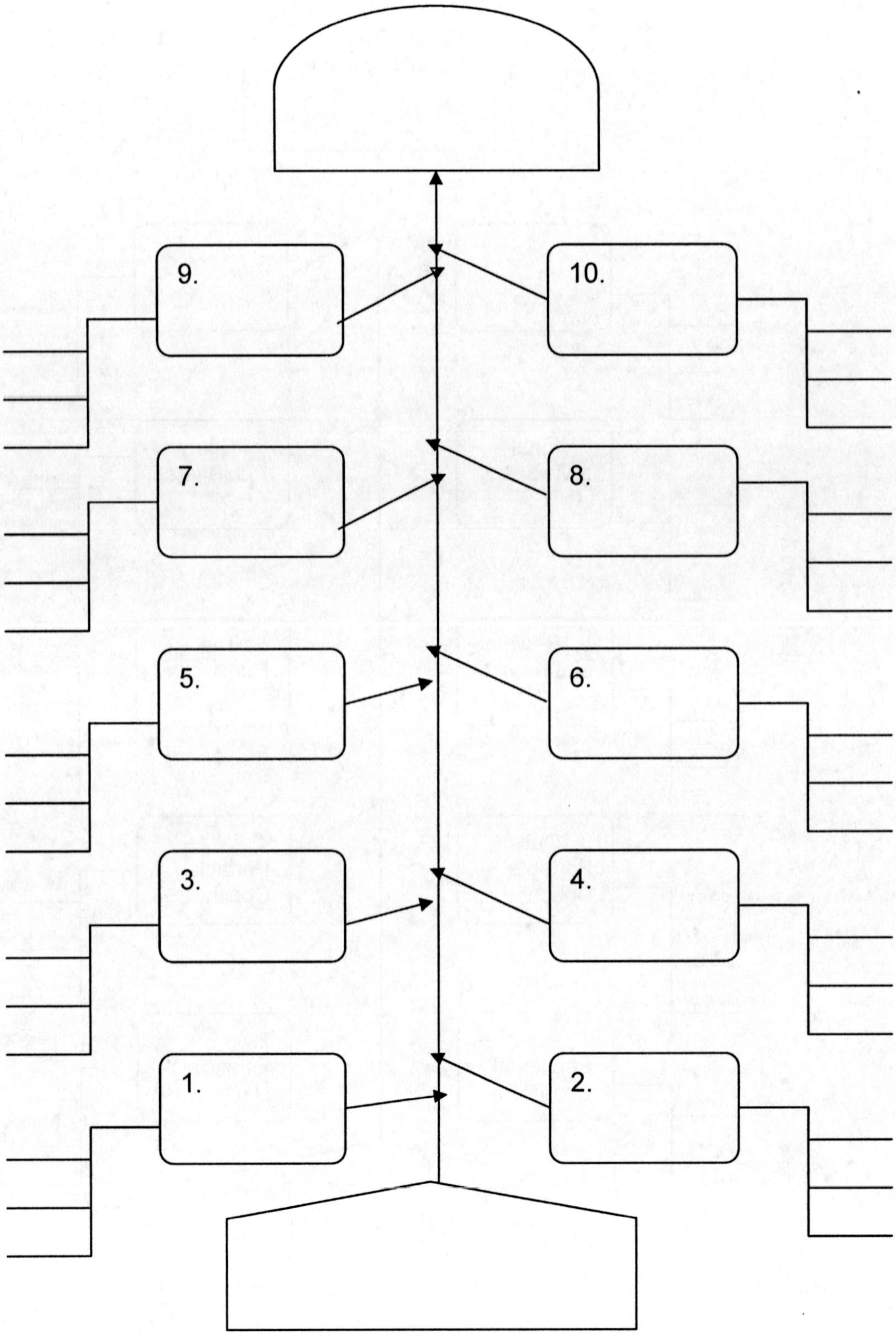
9.
10.
7.
8.
5.
6.
3.
4.
1.
2.

When I first started planning my goals, I was surprised at how manageable they became. I didn't have to change the world in one huge leap, I only needed to take small manageable steps. The thought of looking for a new job may seem overwhelming but it's not overwhelming to update your resume, read the classifieds, and network. All of those things are easily accomplishable.

Skill Builder

Begin taking baby steps to accomplish your goal. Make some phone calls, write some letters. Do something that will help you accomplish what you want to accomplish in your life.

Action Plan

Make a list of things you are going to do in the next week to accomplish your goals and do them!

Five Year Plan

Setting time frames for the completion of goals is an important phase of accomplishing them. Giving yourself deadlines helps focus your efforts on accomplishing your goals. My practice is to develop a five year goals plan. This plan includes 6 month goals, 1 year goals, 2 year goals, 3 year goals, 4 year goals and 5 year goals. Five years seems to work for me, but I know people who have established ten and twenty year goals.

For me to reach my goals, I need to establish realistic time frames that give me enough time but not so much time that I procrastinate. Ten years is so far down the line that I have a tendency to write goals and then forget them until I reach the 9 1/2 year point. Five year goals give me more of an impetus to begin. For me five year goals are the biggies, like buying a house. They are things that will take that long to accomplish. I may not be working every day on those goals, but they are there and I do have to work on them now or they won't be reached.

To construct a five year goals list, review the goals list that you made in Section 2 and determine if you really want to achieve all of these goals. Then assign an appropriate time frame for completion.

Now that you have all of your major goals on your five year plan, go to the FishFlows you created and establish time frames for each of the major steps. Then record those on your five year plan. Ideally, for each of your major goals, there should be something that you can accomplish in the next six months. If the goals will really take five years to accomplish you should have to start working on it *now.* If you don't need to begin work now, maybe you've put too much slack into your time frame. If that's the case, then re-establish a time frame.

I've included a chart for recording your goals or you can create your own. I recommend making a copy of your goals list and putting it in a place that you look at regularly. I have mine by the computer and my yearly goals have been recopied onto the front page of my calendar so I can see them every day.

I hate to fail, and seeing those goals every day reminds me that if I don't work on them, they will never get accomplished.

It is a good idea to review your goals list at least every six months and determine if deadlines need to be moved back or forward or if some goals are no longer applicable to your life. Your goals list should be a work in progress.

Six Month Goals	1 Year Goals	2 Year Goals

3 Year Goals	4 Year Goals	5 Year Goals

Congratulations, you've completed your planning document for the next few years of your life? Can't you feel the rush of energy as you think about accomplishing your goals?

A word about time management. I've tried several planners, organizers, and calendars before I found one that suited me. I buy a weekly appointment book to keep track of my life. It fits into my purse and there is enough room on each page to record what I need to. I personalize mine by putting inspirational clippings, cards from my kids, and other mementos between the leaves. I use a paperclip as a bookmark and by March my calendar looks pretty ratty but it's comfortable and functional. You may prefer a pretty desk top organizer or a computerized organizer. I've found that even though I am a computer nerd, the computerized versions don't work for me. I either had to print out every page or I found myself stuttering when asked to make an appointment because I didn't have my calendar.

I also put my goals list into my calendar and cross them off as I accomplish each goal.

Skill Builder

Take time to explore various calendar options. Go to a good book or stationary store and look through the calendars and organizers that are available. Find one that will work for you and put it to use.

Financial Security

Your financial security needs will depend on your situation. Obviously, if you have a family your needs are going to be greater than if you are single. In addition, your financial needs will depend on your comfort zone. If you feel comfortable and know that something will turn up, then go ahead and quit your job with none lined up. However, if you know that such a risky move will land you in a homeless shelter, then keep your job while you look for something more fulfilling. Your beliefs have a tendency to become self-fulfilling prophecies.

When I first began "trusting the universe" and believing that my trust would carry me through, I didn't put much stock in financial planning. I believed that financial planning showed a lack of faith in the universe and that if this was the path I was meant to be on, miracles would occur. That naiveté and lack of planning resulted in my power being turned off, my phone being cut off, and an empty pantry. These are not fun situations when you have two small children to raise. Something did turn up eventually that was better than what I had, but it took a few months of struggling. Those months could have been prevented if I had done some savvy financial planning. I've come to realize that the universe expects us to use our brains and plan for our futures, not just wait until something falls into our laps.

Unfortunately, most of us haven't won the lottery and don't have a Sugar Daddy to support us while we pursue our dreams. Therefore, we need to do one of two things: work full or part time while we pursue our dream, or put our dream on hold while we save enough money to pursue our dream full time.

Explanations:3

Backup plan: This means working while we pursue our dream. It doesn't necessarily mean keeping your current job. You can take a job that pays enough to make the bills but gives you time and energy to pursue your dreams. I did this when I decided to write The Portable Coach. I was working at a stressful job and although I only worked 40 hours a week I'd come home every night and yell at my kids and fight with my husband. I was not a nice person to be around. The turning point came when I was admitted to the hospital with abdominal pain. I was diagnosed with a ruptured ovarian cyst, but I knew that the pain was stress related. I decided to quit. Flipping burgers seemed preferable to working for my current employer. I temped for a while and then was offered a secretarial position. I was highly overqualified but it paid the bills and I had time and energy to write.

Going it alone: This is the dream option, but for most of us it isn't realistic. We need to keep money flowing in, because hopes and dreams don't pay the electric company. This option is doable if you are single and aren't supporting a family or if you are willing to delay your goals until you save enough money to pursue them full time. The major drawback to this is that a lot of goals we set are fun. They are things we enjoy doing and want to work towards. It's depressing to spend our time and energy doing jobs we hate. If you choose to go it alone, I caution you to plan carefully and ensure your finances are covered.

On the following pages, we'll examine the costs associated with fulfilling your dreams. Don't let the numbers discourage you. There are ways to feed our souls without breaking the bank. Use your creativity to find solutions for seemingly daunting costs.

Start up costs

Because everyone's needs are different, the charts on the following page probably don't cover every cost associated with fulfilling your dreams, so feel free to add any additional costs that you're likely to incur in fulfilling your dreams. I've included space for you to record start-up costs for the materials and supplies you'll need to begin fulfilling your dreams; living expenses that you'll need to ensure are covered; and survival costs to cover extra expenses, if you decide to forego a real job and go it alone.

The following pages contain worksheets for start-up costs for materials and supplies that you'll need to begin accomplishing your goals, living expenses, and survival costs for those of you choosing to go it alone.

Once you've established your costs, I strongly recommend you begin to carefully manage your money. I'm a student of the "Have it and Spend it" school. If I have money in my pocket, I spend it on what I want regardless of what bills I need to pay. I also do a lot of gratuitous spending to improve my emotional state. If finances aren't your strong suit, invest in a budgeting book or a class at a community college. Finances can make or break you. One way that I save money is to let my husband hold on to the extra cash, because his wallet is better than a bank vault.

In analyzing your start-up costs, it's helpful to determine what you need to get started and what you can wait to purchase when money starts rolling in. For instance, my husband and I are starting a computer services business and some of the things that we have in our budget are a scanner, a new computer, and a new printer. However, after analyzing our needs, we realized we could begin typing student papers with the computer we have now and wait to buy a scanner. After we've bought the scanner and the money from scanning starts rolling in, we can upgrade our current computer.

It's also important to consider alternative ways of acquiring things you need, such as buying at thrift shops or bartering for what you need. Second hand stores run the gamut from clothing stores to stores dedicated to second hand computers. This is where creativity rules, find a way to acquire what you need that is within your budget. Use your networking skills to find out if anyone you know has what you're looking for that you could rent or borrow.

Record these items on the following worksheet.

Item:	Be specific about the items you need to fulfill your dreams. Do you need a new computer, a class in water-skiing, or a new tent? Write down all of the things that will help you fulfill your dreams.
Cost:	Do some research to determine how much it's going to cost. Make some phone calls, pick up some catalogs, or get online to do the research.
Need:	Is this something you need immediately or can you obtain it later. I know we all want to rush headlong into fulfilling our dreams, but be honest and realistic. Some things we do need and others can wait.
Other ways to acquire:	Brainstorm to determine if there's a way to obtain this item other than paying full price. Can you barter or go to a second-hand store? Use your creativity to find a way to get what you need.

Start-up Costs

Item	Cost	Need (Immediate or Not)	Other ways of obtaining
Total**			

**This is included to give you an idea of the overall amount you are looking at but don't let it depress you. For a lot of endeavors you can begin on a lot less.

Skill Builder

Choose one of the least expensive items on your list and take action to acquire it. Sign up for a class that you need or purchase an inexpensive item you need and can use immediately. Each small action you take on your dreams makes them more real!

Monthly Expenses

These are the day-to-day survival costs, including food, rent or mortgage, utilities, auto expenses, clothing, etc. I've included entertainment as a survival cost because I've learned that not indulging my playful side is more expensive in the long run than allowing myself small indulgences. If I don't allow myself a little time and money to have fun, I end up going nuts and spending more than I can really afford. I'm not advocating going on a week long trip to Hawaii to alleviate boredom but an afternoon at a local zoo or museum with your family can do wonders for your disposition.

When calculating your day-to-day expenses, take a hard look at where your money is going and determine if there are any ways to save money. Living Off the Employment Grid, co-authored with my husband John, provides a wealth of tips for both saving money and making extra money.

On the following worksheet record the following:

Expense: I've included some daily expenses, but include others that are unique to your situation.

Current Cost: How much are you currently spending on this item per month. Record these costs realistically, because a lot of us have leaks in our wallet and we're not sure where all of our money went at the end of the month. A good way to plug this leak is to record every single expenditure and tally them at the end of the month.

Reduced Cost: What can you reduce this cost to? Would moving into a smaller house cost less money? Determine your minimum survival costs and record them here.

Notes: Record the actions you're going to take to reduce your expenditures and then take action.

Monthly Expenses

Item	Current Expenses	Reduced Expenses	Notes
Rent or Mortgage			
Utilities			
Natural Gas			
Electric			
Phone			
Cable			
Water/Trash			
Internet			
Auto Expenses			
Car Payment			
Gas			
Maintenance			
Tolls			
Insurance			
Groceries			
Eating Out			
Entertainment			
Clothing			
Totals			

Survival Budget

If you choose to go it alone without a job, I recommend that you save at least six times your monthly expenses to live on. This will ensure you can pay your bills while you pursue your dreams. In addition, you'll need to include allowances for such things as medical expenses and catastrophes. When you are working and your car breaks down or an unexpected expense arises, it's possible to juggle bills and ensure that you stay on your feet. It gets harder to juggle those expenses when there is no regular source of income. I recommend a catastrophe fund of at least enough to fix your car, pay a doctor, etc.

The following short work sheet will help budget for those expenses. Include the type of expense, an amount, and an explanation of what you are budgeting for. For instance, medical can mean covering six months' insurance, or ensuring you can meet the cost of a doctor's visit. These are your choices to make, so please make sure they are choices you can live with.

Expense	Budgeted Amount	Explanation
Monthly Expenses (as determined by the previous exercise)		
Medical Care		
Car repair/replacement		
Total		

An encouraging word

Don't get discouraged over these expenses. Finances or the lack of them are not the sole factor in determining if your dreams survive or die. The lack of finances just means you have to work a little harder. My husband is starting a computer consulting business and before we had the funds to acquire our computer, he began taking classes and reading books while we searched for a way to finance the computer. My hated secretarial job provided the answer. The company I work for has a computer purchase program. I got to buy the computer and pay for it over two years out of my paychecks. The best part is that there is a buyout clause that lets me pay the balance of the computer off when I have the funds.

Organizational Skills

In order for you to make your dreams a reality, you'll need to reduce some of the clutter in your life. I know that this is easier said than done but think about how wonderful it feels to sit in a nice clean room. How wonderful it is to open a drawer and be able to find what you need without pulling out every piece of paper in the drawer. There are many wonderful books on organizational skills (see the Resources Section for some suggestions), but I will give you a few tips here:

- If you haven't used something in a year and it has no sentimental value—get rid of it.
- Invest in organization tools such as closet organizers and drawer organizers. These can be expensive but are well worth it.
- Open your mail over the garbage can and get rid of all junk and unused material on the spot.
- Keep tickler files to remind you of things that need to be done. These are sold in office supply stores and come with a slot for each day of the month or a slot for each month. Put things in the appropriate place and forget about them until that day arrives.
- Make to-do lists and cross things off as you accomplish them. There is a wonderful feeling about crossing things off a list.
- Designate a time to return all phone calls. If you are busy, let the machine pick it up and return the call later.
- Get a large calendar for your family and assign each person a different color marker. Record all appointments on the calendar. Older children can be responsible for their own activities. If it's not on the calendar it doesn't get done.
- Learn to say no. We all have a tendency to take on more worthwhile activities that we can do. If it is not extremely important to you, just say NO!!
- Take time for yourself. Taking time to do something you enjoy may seem selfish, but it's a way to recharge your batteries and will give you more energy for the rest of your responsibilities.

Skill Builder

On the lines below, make a list of areas of your life that need organization and begin taking steps to get organized. Clean a drawer, clean a closet, or even clean your car. The first step is the hardest but after that your momentum will keep you going!

Steps to Organization

Emotional Checklist

Before taking action to achieve your goals, it's important to assess your emotional health. I've stormed out of situations angry and lived to regret it, because I'll never know if I gave myself every opportunity I could to succeed. Taking action to change your life is difficult and it is more difficult if you aren't emotionally prepared to deal with the change.

Controlled anger can be a good motivator and can force us to assess our true feelings about a situation, however anger run amuck can lead to stress and shattered relationships. Ideally, those you are dealing with should not be aware of how angry you are in a given situation. As difficult as it is, a decision made in anger should not be acted on in anger. I was in a position that I had been unhappy with for several months when I received my final review. The low scores I received in some areas were justified but others weren't. My boss failed to acknowledge my creativity and initiative in my review and I received a substandard raise. I forced myself to resist telling him to go to hell and storming out of the building. I very calmly, almost too calmly, signed the review and terminated the discussion. I went home, thought about everything that had happened in the last few months and realized it was time to quit. I wrote my resignation letter. The next morning, I dressed in "power clothes" and turned in my resignation. My boss said he had realized the night before that I had reached some kind of decision, but he hadn't expected my resignation. I congratulated myself on holding my temper and not acting rashly. I explained to him that although the review was the catalyst, the decision to leave had been made months before.

When you've made your decision and are prepared to act on it, you should feel at peace with the decision and all the possible consequences. That's how I felt when I left the aforementioned job. I knew it was time to leave and acted on the decision. I was at peace with myself and felt I'd made the decision that was best for me. That peace gave me the courage to carry out the decision.

Making a decision can leave you with a sense of security. You may be leaving something comfortable behind but you are moving on to new and better things. This sense of security has to come from within.

A good decision should leave you with a sense of excitement about the new and different things you will be encountering. You may also feel sadness but the general sense should be one of excitement over the new horizons you will be facing.

Emotional Review

In the space below, record how you feel about the path you are about to embark on. Now is the time to let it all hang out and record your fear, your anger, and your excitement.

Review

Review what you've recorded. If your response is negative and full of an "I'll show them" attitude, it may be necessary to reassess the timing of your decision. Are you really ready to change for yourself or are you making a change in response to someone else? Remember you should be changing for yourself, not to "show" anyone anything. However, if it is a change you truly want to make, the knowledge that you'll be proving someone wrong can be an added incentive to remind you of how much you want this on the days when things aren't going so well.

The only exception of not acting on negative emotions should be if your physical or mental health is being seriously endangered by your current situation. Then get out as fast as you can.

Attitude Builder

If you find you're making a change for someone else, take a look at what benefits you'll get by making the change. Start thinking about changes in your life from your perspective and not from the perspective of other people. Remember: this is your life!

The Company You Keep

The company you keep is important as you begin your journey of change. Positive, supportive people can make reaching your goals easier, but negative people will make it difficult or impossible. Sadly, our families are often the most negative people around. They don't believe that we can accomplish anything out of the norm. We are expected to perform within set roles within set limitations. When we try to break out of this, they put us down and discourage us.

The other type of difficult people are the *enablers*. These are the people that excuse our mistakes, our bad behavior, and enable us to wallow in delusion and self-pity. These are the people that will tell you, "Sure, you can fly on the next space shuttle," regardless of the fact you are 50 pounds overweight, not signed up with NASA, and the next flight is in a month. They excuse our self-destructive behavior and refuse to hold us accountable for our mistakes. I know all about Enablers because I've had plenty in my life. I believe in supporting and helping your friends, but there comes a time when destructive behaviors need to become unacceptable. In addition, enablers cannot or will not give you a dose of reality.

Everyone who encourages you is not an enabler. There are people who can give you healthy, loving, realistic support. They are the people that read your first attempt at a novel and give you constructive criticism. An enabler will tell you your book will make the best seller list in six weeks, a negative person proclaims it the worst piece of trash he's ever read, but a realistic, supportive friend will give you balance. They will support you without giving you false hope.

In addition, be aware that the people you love may be so focused on their own goals that they unintentionally sabotage yours. I have to confess that I have not always been supportive of my husband's efforts to start a Web design business a few years ago when we only had one computer. I was terrible about hogging the computer and not letting him have it to do his work. Luckily, we now have two computers so it's a little easier for us both to work toward our goals.

On the following page, you're going to assess your friends, relatives, and acquaintances and come up with possible comebacks for their putdowns. This exercise will prepare you for the naysayers and enablers.

Reaction Assessment

Record the following information on this worksheet:

Person: Include all of the people in your life that you plan to share your goals with.

Reaction: Get inside their heads and record their imagined response.

Response: How will you respond to their put downs or praise?

Person	Reaction	Your Response

Skill Builder

Use the information recorded to determine who you're going to share your dreams with and who you'll keep in the dark. Learn to be noncommittal. If someone asks sarcastically if you've given up on your dreams, reply that you're still in the planning stage and change the subject. Don't give people the opportunity to put you down. Grab a close friend and practice your responses to put downs. You don't have to lower yourself to a bully's level but don't let them get to you. Politely but firmly let them know that you won't be intimidated.

Networking

Networking is a time honored way to make connections and advance your career in the business world, but networking can help anyone achieve their goals. I define networking as choosing to associate with people who have similar goals and/or people who have already achieved what you are striving for. Networking isn't about using people as much as it is about sharing what you have learned and being willing to learn from others.

Although when you first start networking you might be the one doing all the receiving, as you start accomplishing your goals, you'll find others asking for your advice. The Internet is a wonderful way to meet like-minded people. I belong to several writers' groups and the interaction not only provides me with concrete solutions to problems, it also reminds me that there are other people out there who love to write as much as I do.

Commitment

Sometimes, it's hard to commit to ourselves. We convince ourselves that "We don't deserve this," because other things are more important. The one thing that can make or break your quest for your goal is your level of commitment. If you don't really want this and are not really committed, then it won't happen. You have to believe that you can change your life.

I know that it's scary to commit to this big long term goal. But you can commit to each of the steps. If your goal is to buy a house, it's easier to commit to calling realtors for interviews than it is to commit to buying a house. All you need to do is keep committing to the short term actions and they will add up to the attainment of your goal.

In the space below write three things that you can do within the next week to accomplish one of your goals:

1. ______________________________

2. ______________________________

3. ______________________________

Now mentally commit to accomplishing those things. Put them on your calendar and do them. Once you've completed those three things, check them off and then pick three more things. That's how simple it is. Just take little baby steps and commit to doing the little things. Seeing the check marks on those little things will make it that much easier to do the "big" things.

When I decided to write a book on how people could change their lives, it seemed like a big unmanageable project. I committed myself to writing an outline. Once the outline was done, I committed myself to doing one of the things on the outline. The more I did, the more I found I could do. I promise that's how it will be for you.

Summary

By now your bags should be bulging at the seams and you should be excited about taking the first steps to accomplish your goals. Here's a quick review of what should be in your bags:

- **A list your past accomplishments** to remind you of what you have accomplished in the past and what you will accomplish in the future.
- **Letters of Reference** to remind you that other people think you are a talented and intelligent individual capable of greatness.
- **Disaster Plan** to help you deal with disaster if it strikes.
- **FishFlows** to remind you what steps you need to take to accomplish your goals.
- **Five Year Plan** to remind you when you need to start taking action.
- **Financial Plan** to remind you of how you need to spend and save your money in order to reach your goals.
- **Emotions** game plan to remind you that you can control your emotions and to help you act from a position of strength.
- **A list of friends to trust with your dreams and a list of those to avoid sharing with** to remind you that there are people you can count on and to remind you how to respond when someone puts you down.
- **Commitment** is the most important thing in your bag. Without your commitment to yourself, nothing will get accomplished.

Record your thoughts on Section 3. What steps have you begun to take to make changes in your life?

Slugging it out

You've packed your bags, picked your destination and are ready to depart on your journey to change when you realize you're afraid to take the first step. The more you think about it the more terrified you become. Guess what? If you've been following my suggestions, you've already taken the first step. The image builders and skill builders in the previous sections were designed to get you over the hurdle of that first step. Now that you've taken the first step, the next one should be easier.

As simple as this sounds, it is by no means easy to keep the faith on your journey. Things will go wrong and you will want to hurry back to the comfort of the past. I've been there and I know it's not easy. When I quit my last job to go back to work for a temp agency, I found that the company didn't have many assignments and then my paychecks started bouncing. I ended up in a financial bind and part of me desperately wanted to find a secure auditing or accounting job and settle down. I was desperate but I didn't want to settle for a job that wouldn't give me the time or energy to fulfill my dreams. I went to work for another temp agency and began to catch up on my bills. Then I landed a better paying job that allowed me to work on fulfilling my dreams and keep the bills paid. Hang in there, eventually things will start going your way.

It's when you're ready to give up that you need to pull out your reference letters and lists of accomplishments to remind yourself that you can make it through this hurdle just as you've made it through hurdles in the past. A college friend of mine would say when things got rough, "What are they going to do, take away my birthday?" At the time I didn't understand, but it finally dawned on me that no one can take away who I am. Things might get rough and you may end up homeless and penniless but no one can take away your soul.

The military tried very hard to take away who I was. They broke into my home, arrested me on trumped up charges, and tried to humiliate me. I refused to be humiliated. I knew I had done nothing wrong and that they were trying to terrorize me into leaving Okinawa because of my religious beliefs. I fought my arrest and let them drag me up a hill kicking and screaming. I was prouder of resisting than of almost anything else that I have done. I knew I was right and I wasn't going to let them take away who I was. I didn't let them take away my birthday. No one can take away who you are. You can give it up through passivity, but no one can take it from you.

Keeping the Faith

Throughout this workbook, I have tried to keep my religious viewpoints from coloring what I've written. I don't want this to become an advertisement for my religion, but I do need to say something about Faith. Faith is a belief in yourself and the world. It's a belief that good things will happen eventually. Faith is what gets you up in the morning believing that today will be a better day. Some times it's hard to keep believing but it's during the rough times that it's most important to keep your faith.

I have a personal relationship with my higher power and I pray throughout the day. Sometimes, they are little prayers like "please let my car make it to work." Other times I pray for bigger things. My prayers aren't always of the gimme variety, I also say thanks for the blessings I've received. The most important thing is to keep the lines of communication open.

I've learned that most things happen for a reason and I get in trouble when I force my will on the world. For instance, my husband and I entered into a rent to own option on a fixer upper. I liked the house but I met the landlord and took an instant loathing to him. My gut said to turn and run. I overruled my gut instincts and the deal turned out to be a disaster.

In another instance, my family and I were on Okinawa and were planning to drive up to Peace Park which was about 40 miles away. I went to the ATM the morning before we were to leave and the machine ate my card. I called the bank and found I couldn't get it back until Monday. I contemplated cashing a check at the Officer's club but my gut instincts said this trip was ill fated. The following Monday, I was driving to work and the transmission went out on my car. If I would have pushed forward and gone to Peace Park, my husband and I would have been broken down on the side of the road with a two year old.

Listen to your instincts and trust yourself and whatever higher power you believe in. If you believe that the world is a good place, good things will come to you.

No matter what our religion, we all participate in the rituals of everyday life. We tuck our kids in with a kiss on the forehead at night, we enjoy the paper with a cup of tea. Rituals are a pleasant way to remind our subconscious of what is about to take place. We can create goal rituals too. Perhaps, a special time to review our goals progress. Light a candle and put on some relaxing music and you have the makings of a first class ritual. I use candles and soft music to remind myself that I am a worthy person and I am worthy of success. Take the time to pamper yourself.

We can make our prayer time a ritual by adding candles and incense. Choose candle colors that reflect your needs. Green candles for money, red candles for passion, blue candles for peace or pink candles for love. Choose colors that symbolize your goal and as you light them ask for the power to achieve your goal. Take some time to visualize yourself successfully accomplishing your goals.

Inspiration

One thing that I use to keep my faith is a collection of quotations that I've collected. As I'm reading, I'll come across quotations from people in the past who have toughed it out. These remind me of the universality of my problems and keep me going. A favorite says "Things turn out best for people who make the best of the way things turn out." I remember this when I start whining about all of the problems in my life. By collecting quotations from people who've made it though tragedies and the ordinary struggles of humanity, we remind ourselves that other people have made it. We will too.

One of the men I admire most in the world is John Walsh. His six year old son was murdered in Florida several years ago. Instead of letting this horrendous tragedy destroy his life, he began speaking out to school-aged kids about how to keep themselves safe. He also started the show "America's Most Wanted." By profiling criminals from across the country, citizens are given the opportunity to turn them in. John Walsh, to me, is the epitome of how someone can turn a horrendous personal tragedy into something positive. Although he will never get his son back, his TV show has helped capture hundreds of criminals, and Wal-Mart's "Code Adam," named after his son, has prevented countless more abductions.

I recommend index cards or a Rolodex for your quotations. Put one quote on each card and flip through them when you are in need of inspiration. Keep a few in your pocket or purse and in your car. They'll be there to inspire you when you need them. I know that my collection has kept me going.

I gather sayings from magazines, quote books, and calendars. You can gather wisdom from television shows or movies or from your children. Children are a great source of wisdom and inspiration.

Write your favorite quotes on the following page.

My Favorite Quotes

Affirmations

Affirmations have gotten a lot of publicity in the past several years as a tool of the new agers. Guidance says to tell yourself you already have what you want to acquire. By putting it into the present tense your subconscious will work to create your dreams. I've never found it to be that simple but I do believe affirmations are a wonderful tool if used properly. The best affirmations to use are ones you can believe in. An individual living in a homeless shelter wouldn't be successful using the affirmation "I live in a mansion," because that isn't something they really believe can happen. However, the affirmation "I have my own comfortable place," will ***help*** them achieve what they need. Notice, I italicized the word Help for a reason, I believe that affirmations are tools to be used in addition to more congenital and concrete methods. Sitting in a room and repeating affirmations all day won't get you anywhere unless you also make phone calls, write resumes, and take other real world action. You have to start with something your subconscious can believe. Once you've accomplished your initial goal, move on to other things.

I use affirmations to affirm that I will be given what I need in this life. One of my favorite affirmations is, "I will be provided with what I need." For me this means that the people, circumstances, and things that I need to learn from will be provided for me. My needs will be provided for and I will go on. Another affirmation I use when dealing with difficult people is, "He is a worthwhile person." This reminds me to see the other person as worthy of my respect.

Some affirmations for you to think about

I have ample material possessions.
I live comfortably.
I am at peace with myself.
I love myself and my surroundings.
I am smart, intelligent and worth knowing.

I've found that the affirmations that work for me are ones that concentrate on who I am and not what I have. By making myself happier with who I am, I get more of what I want. I've learned that how I feel about myself makes a real difference in what possessions I have.

Write your favorite affirmations in the space below and refer to them as needed.

Visualization

Another technique I use on a regular basis is visualization. Before I have an interview, or give a presentation, I practice in my mind. I see myself performing well and with confidence. For instance, while I wrote The Portable Coach I visualized myself autographing copies at a bookstore.

Athletes use visualization as well. In written interviews a number of gymnasts, figure skaters, skiers, and divers have stated that before an event they visualize their entire performance in their minds. They mentally practice all of their moves. When the time comes to actually perform, their subconscious recalls the mental rehearsal and their performance is executed flawlessly.

To begin visualizations, find a quiet place and close your eyes. Then using your imagination, play a mental tape of yourself performing well. See yourself getting up in front of a large crowd and giving a speech. See yourself sitting in front of a computer writing your book. Whatever you want to accomplish, visualize your successes. As you practice, you will be able to call these visions to mind when you need them.

A related technique that I use is dream programming. Before I go to sleep I start my visualization and let it carry over into my dreams. I will my dream body to accomplish what I want my physical body to do. I've found that both of these techniques ease the nervousness the real world sometimes brings to events.

In the space below, write a script for your visualization. Write down what you want to see as the video replays in your head. This will make it easier to replay in your mind. The first few times you try visualizing, reread what you've written to give yourself a script. Then let your imagination take off. Stop your freestyle visualization if you find yourself visualizing failure. Force yourself to restart the tape and visualize success.

Make changes to your script as need be and remember you are a winner!!

Wishing Boards

Similar to visualization is what my family calls "Wishing Boards." These give a physical visual presence to your visualizations. We make wishing boards once a year and hang them up to remind ourselves of what we want to accomplish. To make a wishing board, get a large piece of poster board, collect photos that represent your goals, both tangible and intangible, and paste them on in any arrangement that suits you.

If your goal is to be thin, collect pictures of fashion models dressed in wonderful clothes and paste a picture of your head on their bodies. If your goal is to have lots of friends, collect pictures of people doing "friend things" and put them on your board. Let your imagination run wild.

I always use magazine photos when putting together my Wishing Boards because I'm a poor artist. If you are more artistically inclined, feel free to put your own drawings on your board

After you've completed your Wishing Board, hang it in a place you'll see every day. The effect of the pictures on your subconscious is tremendous. Your mind will take over from there and push you towards what you see in the pictures. It works amazingly well. One of my goals for last year was to lose weight and get fit. I placed a photo of a woman running away from the camera on my wishing board but didn't put any frontal views. Within six months, my backside was trimming up but my front wasn't.

Look at your boards often and begin taking real world action towards obtaining your goals.

Map it Out

We've created FishFlows to plan our progress, now it's time to create a road map complete with stepping stones to mark out as we progress down the road. The principle is similar to crossing days off on a calendar or opening the doors on an advent calendar. A road map will present you with a succinct picture of where you are at any given point.

To make a roadmap, create a beginning and an ending point on a piece of paper. These can be circles, stars, whatever you would like. Then draw a road between the points, it's best to make the road long and curvy so that you have enough room to cross off all of your steps. Now, take your FishFlow and your goals list and create a master lists of steps to your goal. Then count these steps and partition your road into this many steps. As you accomplish each step, color in that step on your map.

You can either write in what the step is on your map or put numbers on your map showing how many steps you've accomplished. When I wrote The Portable Coach, I counted how many sub sections of the book I was going to write, revisions I anticipated, etc., and then numbered the steps in my map. I didn't assign each step a particular number because I wasn't sure of the order I would accomplish them in. I just counted the steps I had completed and colored that many squares

Some additional notes. For roadmaps, divide your project into small, easily accomplishable steps. This means you can color them in easily and you'll see progress more rapidly. Your roadmap should be in a place that is easily accessible to you no matter what. I carried the map for The Portable Coach in my purse while I was working on it. Then I could color in those squares as soon as I finished them. Your road map should be a cheery welcoming place so add some trees, clouds, flowers and the sun. I've included a sample road map for you to fill out.

Draw your Road Map Here

Procrastination

Procrastination can be a double-edged sword: sometimes we procrastinate because we are fearful and other times we procrastinate because we know in our heart of hearts that the path we are contemplating is not right for us.

Procrastination can be a real goal killer. Sometimes, we procrastinate because we are afraid of accomplishing our goals and being successful. I wrote the outline for The Portable Coach and let it sit for several weeks because I was afraid that once I'd written the book it wouldn't be any good. I was finally motivated enough to get started and I finished the first four sections in two weeks. It took another three weeks to finish the last section because I let my fear stand in my way.

One of the best pieces of advice I ever heard was, "Anything worth doing is worth doing badly." In other words, make an attempt at your project and then rework it as necessary. The thrill of actually accomplishing something will motivate you to redo it until it becomes a masterpiece.

I took this advice to heart while I was finishing The Portable Coach, I forced myself to sit down and write. A lot of what I wrote those last few days was really bad but I forced myself to get it out on paper. At least my thoughts would be on paper and I'd have a starting block for rewrites. That's the advantage of doing something badly: a place to start.

As you near completion of your goal, force yourself to take those final steps and get it done. Don't let procrastination rob you of the pleasure of reaching your goals.

The flip side of procrastination is that sometimes we are contemplating a course of action because "it is the right thing to do." We don't really want to do something but feel we must. For instance, I contemplated going back to school to get my MBA for several years but I found one excuse after another. I finally realized that I really didn't want an MBA.

In the space below, record instances where you have procrastinated and analyze whether the procrastination has been because of fear or a deep seated feeling that your chosen path was not right:

Procrastination	Analysis

From reviewing the above information, review your next instance of procrastination and determine if it is fear or reluctance to undertake a goal. If it is fear, begin taking baby steps toward your goal. If it is reluctance, analyze your goals and determine whether they are really right for you.

Party Time

One of the most important steps on your journey to your goal is to celebrate your successes. As you take significant actions toward meeting a goal, congratulate yourself and treat yourself to a special reward. It can be dinner and a movie or the purchase of a special book you've been wanting. Each step you take is an accomplishment to be praised. You needn't plan a large celebration for every minor step but do take the time to congratulate yourself on being that much closer to your goals. Celebrate the accomplishment of the major steps of your goals by treating yourself, but make sure that your treat doesn't interfere with accomplishing your goal. For instance, if you're trying to lose weight, don't reward yourself for losing 10 pounds with a hot fudge sundae! Appreciating yourself helps you take the next steps and makes your goals that much more tangible.

Skill Builder

In the space below, plan your blowout. Write down who you are going to invite, where your party's going to be held, and what food you are going to serve. Write down all the details and when the going seems rough, remind yourself of the fantastic party you have planned.

My Celebration Party

Course Corrections

I wouldn't be honest with you if I told you that you will meet every goal you set. If you make an honest effort to meet your goal and you cannot achieve it, applaud yourself for making the effort. I consider failure a lack of effort, not a lack of results. Enjoy and be grateful for what you've learned. I interviewed for an auditing position that would have been perfect for me. It was in a great location, the travel wasn't too bad and the company was a Fortune 500 company. They paid all of my travel expenses including a hotel room for my husband and I the night before the interview. My goal was to present myself in a professional manner and give a good interview. My secondary goal was to enjoy the time with my husband out of our normal setting of kids and dogs. I walked away from the interview knowing I had given one of my best interviews. I didn't get the job, but I had a nice weekend with my husband and I proved to myself that I could interview well. I reminded myself that out of hundreds of applicants for the position, I was one of the eight they chose to interview. That in and of itself was an accomplishment.

Part of transforming your life is to be open to new ideas and new paths. Once you begin the journey, you never know what you will encounter along the way. Some of the side roads are more interesting than the main road. It's like taking a trip and making time to explore the side roads. Life is a journey, not a destination. Remember that.

On the following pages, we're going to analyze your goals and determine why you didn't meet the goal. We'll look at what if anything was learned in the attempt. If you no longer believe a goal is valid, feel free to record that in your notes section.

Goal Evaluation

Many people set goals and forget about them until one day they pull out a piece of paper and are reminded of another goal not met. At the other end of the spectrum are the people who spend so much time obsessing about what they want to accomplish that they never accomplish anything. The middle ground is to periodically reevaluate your goals and make course corrections as necessary. I review and revise my goals every three to six months. During this review, you may decide to leave your upcoming goals as they stand or you may revise your goals list. The following worksheet will help you to evaluate your goals

Record the following:

Goal:	A short description of the goal.
Target Date:	Your original target date.
Progress:	Notes on progress you have made toward your goal. This should include obstacles you've encountered as well as what success you are enjoying. If you are going to abandon your goal, record that here.
Revised Target:	If necessary, record a revised target date.

Exercise—Goal Analysis

Goal	Original Target Date	Progress	Revised Target Date

Goal	Original Target Date	Progress	Revised Target Date

Analysis

This exercise should have given you an idea of what goals you need to reevaluate. Be realistic and realize that revising deadlines is not a failure: it is only a reevaluation. We don't live in a perfect world and circumstances arise which are out of our control. Sometimes it is necessary to rethink where we are and where we are going. If you find yourself going through major life changes, it might be helpful to rework some of the exercises in Sections 1 through 4.

Setting and evaluating goals is a learning process. Many times, we learn more from the goals we fail to meet than the goals we accomplish. I've learned much more about myself and about life from my disappointments than through my triumphs. We don't always realize what lessons we've learned until we look back and realize that what appeared to be a disaster was a blessing in disguise.

Lessons from the Trenches

As I said before, the lessons that we've learned from past disappointments aren't always readily apparent. When I graduated from college and took a job with the U.S. Air Force, it was my intention to have a long lasting career with the government. My career was over within six years and at the time I was bitterly disappointed and angry. Looking back I see that if I had continued working for the government, I would never have gained the self confidence that I have now. I wouldn't be pursuing my dreams of writing: I would be a government drone.

On the following pages, you're going to review some of your disappointments and see if you can find a pearl in the oyster. These do not have to be goals that you have set for yourself in the course of working through this workbook. They can be childhood or early adult. These goals should, however, be serious goals that you have made an effort to reach.

For each of the record the following:

Goal:	What was the goal you wanted to reach?
Why you didn't reach the goal:	Did you not reach your goal due to external circumstances or was it through a lack of planning?
What would you do differently?	Hindsight is always 20/20. Was there anything you could have done differently that may have enabled you to reach your goal?
What have you learned?	What did you learn from your disappointment?
Feelings about outcome:	Are you proud of your effort? Was your lack of success a blessing in disguise?

Exercise—Lessons from the Trenches

Goal	Why you didn't attain?	What would you do differently?

Goal	What have you learned?	Are you glad?

Analysis

In reviewing your answers to the above questions, I hope that you've found at least some of your personal disasters to be blessings in disguise. Did you turn down a dream job only to have the company go bankrupt in six months? Did you turn down a trip to Europe only to meet your dream partner in New York? Life has a funny way of working out for the best.

Next time you begin to feel down over your lack of success, review your notes and realize that in several months you'll see the silver lining. I like to think of myself as a "human becoming" instead of a "human being." Life is a process and there is always something new to learn.

Review

The processes I've outlined in this book are a never-ending spiral. They can be applied at any time in your life and to any goal. Take what you've learned the first time through and apply it the next time you set goals. You are creating your own roadmap to the future. A lot of things happen that are upsetting at the time but looked at with hindsight are blessings.

Next time you want to set goals, remember to:

- ☯ Take the time to determine who you are today. In subsequent years this process won't be as time-consuming as it was the first time through, but it's important to periodically review your strengths and weaknesses.
- ☯ Set appropriate, realistic goals.
- ☯ Pack your self esteem, appropriate finances, and a good dose of friends.
- ☯ Encourage yourself with the tricks listed here when the going gets rough.
- ☯ Periodically reevaluate your goals and determine if they are still valid for your life.

I wish each and every one of you luck on your journey through life.

Notes on The Portable Coach

My Story

I stated in my opening paragraphs that I'd been disappointed by a lot of self-help books I've read. The solutions seemed too easy and it made me wonder if the authors had really had success with their methods. I'd like to tell you that I have had success with the steps I've outlined. It has been a long and at times unpleasant journey but I'm finally seeing the finish line.

I started working through the prototypes of these exercises in 1993 after my family and I came back from Okinawa. I realized that my life was at a crossroads and I had to make a decision as to what path to take. Part of me wanted to become part of corporate America with a regular job, a mortgage, and two weeks vacation. That path would have been very easy to take. My spirit didn't want that. I've always been an adventurer.

Analyzing who I was was difficult. I found that I was ashamed of many of my possessions and I thought people looked down on me because of what I possessed. Talk about low self esteem. At the time I was driving a ten year old car and I "heard" people snickering wherever I went. I didn't fit my definition of success. I finally realized that people with brand new cars were generally paying $300 a month in car payments for the privilege of driving that car. In order to keep the car and all of the other possessions, they had to stay on the treadmill. My husband and I, on the other hand, have made a conscious effort to live within our means. Our bills are easily covered by one salary, which gives us the security of knowing that the loss of one job won't mean that we'll end up homeless and penniless.

I knew that I wanted to be a writer and the first year back from Okinawa I wrote my first novel, sure that it would be a best seller. It wasn't; I got several rejection letters and reevaluated the book and my talents. I decided that I wanted to write but I wasn't very good at writing fiction. Essays and informational articles were more my forte. I was the kid in school who loved writing research papers.

My common sense told me that in order for me to live the life I wanted to live, I had to identify what made me happy. I began analyzing my fantasies and daydreams to determine what I really wanted out of life. I found I wanted to spend time with my family, write, and have a comfortable life. I don't want to be a miserly millionaire and I don't want a career that requires me to work 80 hour weeks.

Failure has always been my worst fear. I'm afraid that I'll look bad or that I'll make a fool of myself. It took a lot of baby steps before I was ready to declare myself a writer and put my efforts before the world. I finally started submitting articles for publication and I had a few successes and a lot of rejections. The rejections hurt but I refused to let them destroy my dreams.

Over the course of the next few years, I learned emotional control and how to better control my finances. I solicited letters of recommendation from coworkers and friends and began buoying myself with the quotations.

It was about this time that I was voraciously reading self help books. One thing that I realized about all of these books was that they required you to write exercises but never provided a place to write. I hated having to keep the book and my journal together. I always ended up giving up because I'd misplace my journal and have to find another one. I'd have my exercises written in three different books. I decided that I could write a better book than many of the ones I was reading because through my own efforts, I had fashioned a life in which I was comfortable with who I was. Writing hadn't yet become a financial success but I was happy and confident. Maybe the lessons I had learned in my life could help others. I hope these exercises help you make the changes you want to make in your life.

Resources

The following are resources that have helped me as I've made changes in my life. I hope they can provide you with some guidance as well. You can also visit my Website at http://lenos66.com for even more resources.

A 2nd Helping of Chicken Soup for the Soul by Jack Canfield and Mark Victor Hansen. Health Communications, Inc.

A 3rd Helping of Chicken Soup for the Soul by Jack Canfield and Mark Victor Hansen. Health Communications, Inc.

A Winning Attitude: How To Develop Your Most Important Asset by Michelle Fairfield Poley. Skillpath Publications

Applied Imagination by Alex Osborn. Charles Scribner's Sons

Chicken Soup for the Soul at Work, by Jack Canfield, Mark Victor Hansen, Maida Rogerson, Martin Rutte, and Tim Clauss. Health Communications, Inc.

Chicken Soup for the Soul by Jack Canfield and Mark Victor Hansen. Health Communications, Inc.

Chicken Soup for the Women's Soul by Jack Canfield, Mark Victor Hansen, Jennifer Read Hawthorne, and Marci Shimoff. Health Communications, Inc.

Complete Guide To Making Money With Your Ideas And Inventions by Richard Paige. Prentice Hall

Creative Visualization by Shakti Gawain. MJF Books

Cutting Loose: A Civilized Guide For Getting Out Of The System by Saturday Review Press

How to Want What You Have by Timothy Miller, PhD. Henry Holt and Company

Putting Your Talent to Work by Lucia Capacchione, PhD and Peggy Van Pelt, PhD Health Communications, Inc.

Dreams Of Isis by Normandi Ellis. Quest Books

Encyclopedia Of Associations by Gale Research Company

Establish Yourself As An Authority by Sol H. Marhall. Creative Book, Co.

Finding Facts Fast: How To Find Out What You Want To Know Immediately by Alden Todd. William Morrow

Getting Organized: The Easy Way To Put Your Life In Order by Stephanie Winston. Warner Books

Getting Things Done by Edwin C. Bliss. Bantam

Get Your Act Together: A 7-Day Get Organized Program for the Overworked, Overbooked, and Overwhelmed by Pamela Young. Harper Periennel

If You Don't Know Where You're Going, You'll Probably End Up Somewhere Else by David Cambell. Argus Communications

Reinventing Your Self by Mark Towers. Skillpath Publications

Simply Organized: How to Simplify Your Complicated Life by Connie Cox. Putnam

The Life You Were Born To Live by Dan Millman. Kramer, Inc.

Thriving In Tough Times by Paul G. Fox. Career Press

Totally Organized, the Bonnie McCullough Way by Bonnie McCoullough. St. Martin's Press

Why Me, Why This, Why Now by Robin Norwood. Carol Southern Books

Work With Passion - How To Do What You Love For A Living by Nancy Anderson. New World Library

Printed in the United States
4374